AF256537

# FRONTIERS IN ENERGY MEDICINE

## UNLOCK THE ENIGMA OF ENERGY HEALING

### CAROL ROBERTSON

ENERGY AND PHYSICS – THE NATURAL SCIENCE OF THE WORK WITHIN

Copyright © 2024 Carol Robertson

All rights reserved.

No part of this book may be reproduced in any format or by any mechanical, photographic, electronic process, or recording. Nor may it be stored, transmitted, or otherwise copied for public or private use without the express written permission of the author. It may be utilised for brief excerpts or quotations in articles and reviews subject to a policy of 'fair use.'

There is an old Indian saying which iterates that 'The first and foremost form of happiness is that of having a healthy body'. Good health indeed is a blessing. Yet like a Mirage it can fizzle out. People are bewildered that when they eat right and exercise right, and still, they are at DIS-EASE. I too desperately sought for the cause and solution!

Carol is the best trailer blazer of ACMOS teachings, which incorporates the core values of Indian Ayurveda and Traditional Chinese Medicine and puts forth a new understanding of DIS-EASE. Hereditary issues, ancestral memories, trauma, thoughts, emotions, and geobiological factors all play a role in our wellbeing as much if not more than what we eat and how we exercise.

Carol's new book on the Lecher Antenna lets you dive into this hidden world which accounts for a huge proportion of health-related problems. Since we are talking about energy and its alignment, it is Carol's vibrant energy which would charge up and illuminate your journey of Bioenergetics via this book of hers... Go and grab a copy today!

**Tanuja Singh** *Certified ACMOS Bioenergetics Practitioner*
*Director ACMOS India, Assistant Professor,*
*Registered Yoga Teacher with Yoga Alliance, U.S.*

Learning from Carol has been an amazing experience, in the truest sense of that word. Her immense knowledge in this very advanced ACMOS system has tremendously helped me in my healing journey as well as in my profession. I was looking to incorporate a holistic modality to enhance my practice, and ACMOS fitted right in as its principles are very aligned with that of Ayurveda. Now I can test all the nuances of the Ayurvedic approach by testing with the ACMOS Lecher antenna! It is an amazing modality.

I am very fortunate to have learnt it from Carol Robertson. Her fun, patient and loving personally has made this subject come alive. Although it seems a very technical subject, she has made it so simple and easy to learn with this book, great videos, and amazing Scottish sense of humor.

***Mukta Mudgal*** *Certified ACMOS Bioenergetician*
*Ayurvedic Practitioner and meditation teacher.*
*https://www.healingbymukta.com/About*

You will learn to work with the Body and understand what energies are needed to remove blocks so that the body can balance itself. Since our bodies talk in frequencies and wavelengths, if we learn to listen and interact with these wave signals properly, we can bring about balance which is a potent tool. The ACMOS Lecher antenna is a scientific instrument that provides us this gateway.

My coaching sessions are more powerful now because I can check my clients Bio-Energetic readings before and after a coaching session. The antenna has transformed my life and continues to amaze me with its powers. If you're like me and have had interest in learning different wellness modalities such as energy balancing, quantum healing and others, but feel overwhelmed with the amount of information, time, as well as financial commitments to each one that is required, you should check out the trainings, coaching and community created by Carol Robertson in the world of ACMOS and Bioenergetics!

***Ayda Walsh*** *Certified ACMOS Bio-Energetician*
*Hypnotherapist, EFT Trainer & Practitioner,*
*Certified Master NLP & Life Coach*
*http://hlrad.com/*

# THE INTERNATIONAL ACADEMY OF ENERGETIC HEALTH™ EXISTS TO ENGAGE ENABLE & ENRICH LIVES

We teach Lecher Antenna techniques, profound energy medicine skills, and a holistic view of health based on anatomy, Chinese medicine, and resonance.

We integrate this unique knowledge into ACMOS, a René Naccachian Method, to help us understand the root cause of dis-ease, to explain the unconscious and energetic connections with surface symptoms and to recalibrate the energy body, to restore the person's innate ability to heal.

Carol Robertson is a specialist teacher of The ACMOS Method, a philosophy founded on the principles of resonance & Traditional Chinese Medicine and also a Chartered Physiotherapist with over 30 years' experience.

- *Magnetise the Mind* — we provoke interest and curiosity in learning, presenting information in innovative ways. We from solid foundations in knowledge and analysis techniques.

- *Balance the Body* — we facilitate healing using energetic systems and profound skills to enhance your own health and that of your clients — accessing and retuning the hidden information of our destiny.

- *Satisfy the Soul* — we place the heart and soul, mindful and deeply connected, at the very centre of our work – always!

Whether you are a novice or are already an advanced practitioner, we have creative ideas and courses to help you aspire to new heights and achieve your outstanding potential.

# DISCLAIMER

The information contained within this book allows the user to access information held in the subtle body for personal use.

It does not replace, either directly or indirectly, the need to consult an appropriate medical doctor or specialist to assess, diagnose and treat any physical or mental health problems.

In the event that you make personal choices based on the information held in this book, you do so at your own discretion and the author does not assume any responsibility for your actions.

Please read the book before using the protocol at the end.

# CONTENTS

# FOREWORD

## Frontiers In Energy Medicine – Volume One

*—— John Cross FCSP, Dr Ac*

It is an honour and a privilege to write the Foreword for this book, the first by my good friend and colleague Carol Robertson.

Carol has encountered and overcome many trials and tribulations in her personal and professional life – losing her job to ill-health caused her terrible sadness but she has triumphed over all to produce this excellent book on her specific aspect of energy medicine.

In her professional life as a chartered physiotherapist, she has dared to think 'outside the box'. At times there was ridicule and castigation by her peers as her chosen methods are not 'evidence based' in the western sense. What modern scientific medicine rarely appreciates, though, is that traditional medicine used the science of its day. None of it, whether it is acupuncture, homoeopathy or many other approaches of energy medicine just happened, they were formulated by pioneers who took years (sometimes decades) of painstaking research, trials and empirical evidence before outcomes could be published.

Although modern medicine has introduced many forms of traditional approaches into its fold, one of the main stumbling blocks is its non-acceptance of **vitalism** — upon which most forms of energy medicine are based.

Responsibility for our health has to land fairly and squarely with ourselves, our patients, and our clients. Carol truly understands, as patient, observer, and practitioner, that the natural medicine therapist merely opens certain keys, and changes gears within the patient's own vital force, in order for them to self-heal.

I have become very impressed with the ACMOS method over the past few years as it is truly a non-invasive therapy that balances the patient's energetic fields and aura to re-establish harmony. What makes it really impressive is that it combines traditional medicine with modern molecular biology. If you enjoy the book, why not check out Carol's training courses so that you too may become a practitioner.

John R. Cross Dr. Ac.; FCSP; Author

Isle of Skye – February 2024

John Cross has devoted his life to taking the mystique out of the esoteric energy system, being called a world authority by his peers.

# The ACMOS Lecher Antenna (ALA)

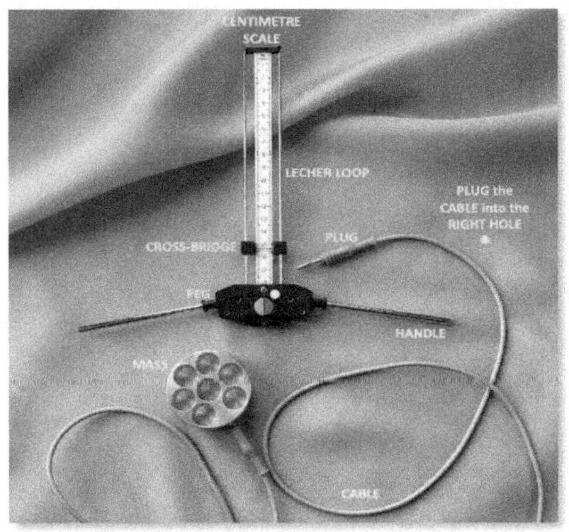


**Lecher loop:**    Tunes in with electromagnetic waves.

**Centimetre scale:**    Accurately locates the important wavelengths.

**Cross-bridge:**    Sliding shunt — varies the length of the Lecher loop.

**Pegs:**    Stabilising pegs fix the handles of the antenna in place.

**Plug:**    Two plug holes for inserting the cable. Use the *right* hole as you face the antenna.

**Mass:**    Metal electrode which is used during testing.

**Cable:**    Connects the mass to the antenna

The antenna, cable, mass, and person create a bio-electrical circuit.

# Chapter One:
## Introduction to Energy in Medicine

Energy medicine or vibrational medicine are becoming more popular around the world, so why do I believe that embracing energy in health is vital?

*Energy is not only essential to health, energy is integral to, and inseparable from health. No energy, no life… period!*

So let's have a quick look at the underpinning logic that supports the use of energy as a term in relation to health and well-being.

### Firstly, what do I mean by energy?

Well, I'm not talking about something esoteric and woo woo or wacky, I am talking about the flow which underlies the natural state we all strive for; physical, mental, emotional, and spiritual health. When any of these aspects of health is out of balance, we do not feel whole, and health according to the roots of language means exactly that, whole. Newer medical definitions emphasize health as, the capacity to adapt to changing external and internal circumstances[1]. We do not live in a vacuum, and we are affected by our internal and our external environment, as well as our familial traits and tendencies. These underlying and acquired programmes affect how we use our energy to grow, develop, and maintain our structure whilst simultaneously managing our emotions. So let's look a little deeper:

---

[1] What is health? Harald Brüssow* Microb Biotechnol. 2013 Jul; 6(4): 341–348. Published online 2013 May 6. doi: 10.1111/1751-7915.12063

The fundamental triad of life on Earth:

1.  The **physical** body – a collective of 50 trillion working cells.

    Our physical structure is a working factory, building, repairing, growing, and eliminating waste products 24 hours per day 365 days per year. The body is always working, even as we sleep our cells, organs and systems are working, and work requires energy.

    We are born of energy – conceived from the energy of two humans, created at the point of nuclear fusion of the egg and the sperm. Throughout our lifetimes we gain energy from the food we eat, and energy from the air we breathe, but we also absorb positive energy directly from sunlight, and connect with the calming nature and negative ions of the earth.

    This combination of work in our bodies, in synergy with the natural forces of nature, starts from the moment of conception and some of this work continues, at a cellular level as the body slows down, after we depart our mortal form.

    *Work – a quintessential aspect of physics.*

2.  The **emotional** body and mind manifest our state of charge, and influence behaviour.

    So what does charge mean in this context? Big emotions carry big charge, whether negative or positive, they create a movement of energy, a change in voltage, which creates or drives a current. As this electrical charge passes through electrically conductive tissues, (the nervous system is a great conductor) it creates a reaction in our structure and continues out as a vibration into our auric fields. So the charge is bigger than the body.

    If you are sensitive you can feel the charge emanating from other people, a charge which fluctuates with their emotional state. In this context, charge relates to bio or living electricity, the electromagnetic effect of thoughts and feelings. The brain is a huge user of energy, but the mind also requires energy in order to function, which creates a charged reaction in our environment. We upregulate and downregulate our nervous system, and our state of charge, as appropriate to each situation. The result is an electromagnetic change, or energetic change, in the nervous system and in the emotional state.

*Managing our emotions requires us to regulate the charge in our body — physics!*

3.  And what of the **vibratory** body?

    Invisible, indetectable to the bodily senses, the vibrations of the soul and the spirit exist as ripples or waves, moving in the spaces within us and around us, mini or macro distortions in the fabric of the universe, and that's physics too.

    Have you ever considered the soul through the lens of physics as the vital force which animates our form with life? The vibration of who we truly are.

    And spirit, the energy from which we came and our connection with all things. A connection that we maintain throughout our lives, and which eventually draws us home to whence we came. Use any name you are comfortable with, there is no denying that there is a unifying force in the universe, a divine order to all things.

But let's go back to the basic sciences — where else does energy, as physics, fit into our understanding of health?

## SPEED

When I learned physics at school, one of the first things I remember learning about was velocity, or speed, but I never thought about the crossover with biology until I started working with energy. The speed at which our body works optimizes its efficiency, and an efficient body, like an efficient machine requires less fuel. In fact, an efficient body will manage its own functions really well, and it will heal itself whenever it can.

## COMMUNICATION

Our senses form the basis of communication – when we communicate there is a transference of information, an exchange of energy. I am a therapist and whenever I meet a new client, we start assessing each other, listening, looking sensing and feeling our interaction. When we look, we are perceiving, and interpreting light waves, and so we see. When we listen, mechanical waves hit our eardrums, we do not only perceive the words, we also hear tone of voice, tightness or charge, we hear and sense changes in emotional state.

Some people can even smell disease. Joy Milne, a Scottish nurse noticed that her husband developed a particular smell 10 years before his Parkinson's diagnosis. Her ability to detect this specific smell led to research, which may result in an early test for Parkinson's disease.

Another example of sensing energetic change in a way which supports wellbeing — dogs can be trained to alert their owners of an impending epileptic fit before anything is felt by the person, or visible to other people. The dogs sense the change in charge and the person can find a safe position before the fit occurs.

Isn't it amazing to have the ability to isolate specific data through the senses? The vibrations and the molecular signals emanating from objects and people, can have measurable and useful applications.

At this point in history, we are struggling to cope with the stress and crises we have faced over the past few years. It is almost as if we are being challenged to raise our vibration. We live in the face of planetary tensions and global events, heat, wind, flooding, and storms – these are the stories of 2023. Global threats put us under pressure, and as a result extreme of natural tensions explode as wars – neighbourhood wars, political wrangling and devastating international wars. Humans have an ancient inbuilt tendency to revert to our innate tribal instincts when we feel under pressure. We blame our neighbours, families, and foes – and if we feel under enough pressure we fight.

To top this new era in human history, our health been particularly challenged by pandemics over recent years. Symptoms of dis 'ease' exacerbated by fears over viral impact, and/or perception of vaccination threat. We have not only lived with Covid and the fears and devastation that brought, but also pandemics of symptoms such as chronic pain, fatigue, depression, and anxiety.

As an example, a staggering 10.1% of the adult population of the world suffer from chronic fatigue – that's 533 million people[2]. And that doesn't count the 79 million young people or those without a diagnosis. The economic effect is staggering £3.5 billion per year in the UK, $20-25 billion in the US but more importantly, the consequences of this global suffering on a personal level are unthinkable.

> *Fear and anxiety are enormous users of energy, so no matter what we believe about the 2020s, the impact on our psyche and our energetics has been huge – and it is ongoing.*

---

[2] The demographic features of fatigue in the general population worldwide: a systematic review and meta-analysis Ji-Hae Yoon et al July 28 2023 Front Public Health. 2023; 11: 1192121

So why is now a good time to embrace the energetic aspects of health?

Now is the time to take care of our 'selves' — to nurture our bodies, sooth our souls, and support our connection with the natural sciences of life. Not only our biology and our biochemistry, but also our biophysics – the influence of the natural energetic forces on all lifeforms, the forces that speed us up and slow us down. The forces that are always present.

Plant-life, animal life, microscopic life, all exist because of sunlight. Our sweet spot in the galaxy means that our sun is not too hot when balanced by the natural defences of the earth. These forces have danced together since before the dawn of life on Earth, and we all exist in a natural balance with the sun's cosmic force and the Earth's telluric force today.

The man-made world of gadgets, mobile phones or wireless communications is simply the result of machines being developed, with the appropriate application of physics, to allow effective transference of information across distance. The Lecher loop predates modern technology by over a hundred years but is no less effective in its task. It is time to explore and connect with the natural physics which allows life to thrive here on earth.

By embracing the physics of life, and using a tool to measure, interpret and recalibrate our energy body, we can be more comfortable, more at 'ease' amid the chaos around us. We can take back a sense of control, of being able to do something to support our wellbeing.

We can measure our connections with the sun and the earth. We can assess the impact of foods, supplements, people, places, and other items, on our energy body. We can influence how we tune in with natures balance, and we can reset our connections, like switching on a light then adjusting the dimmer switch to the most comfortable setting.

If you are interested in the true meanings of words than consider this. The root of the word energy derives from *the work within.* The etymology or root of the word physics is *the natural science* and, as mentioned before, the root of the word health is *whole.*

Health — the natural capacity to adapt to changing external and internal circumstances.

| | | |
|---|---|---|
| *Embrace the natural science of the work within to optimise health.*[©] | = | *Harness the physics of living or bio-energy to enhance wholeness.* |

Energy work is not magical, but neither is it as mysterious as some would have us believe. It is a work in progress.

So what can we do to help ourselves navigate today's plethora of unnatural signals?

Allow me to present to you *the Lecher Antenna* — a tool, a gadget, a scientifically calibrated instrument. An instrument which can open information pathways and find the answers to questions which may not even exist yet. Once called nature's best kept secret (Michael Brooking) the Lecher antenna has a long and distinguished career in radio and television, and now is its time to shine in the wellbeing sector.

# Chapter Two:
# History of the Lecher Antenna

The name Lecher Antenna is attributed to **Ernst Lecher** (1856 – 1926), who was an esteemed physicist at the University of Vienna. The most notable of Lecher's studies focussed on the electro-magnetic propagation of waves along two wires. His innovative studies in this field led to the Lecher Loop being named after him in the early part of the twentieth century. Although a very simple device, this wire loop, with a sliding shunt (cross-bridge) which varied the length of the loop, enabled scientists to tune into electromagnetic waves with great accuracy.

Heinrich Hertz was a pioneer in the use of standing waves to calculate wavelength, however he was unaware of the importance of his discovery of 'mysterious electromagnetic waves' that could not be seen with the naked eye. Initially called Hertzian waves, airborne electromagnetic waves became synonymous with radio waves around 1910.

Sliding a cross-bridge, along parallel wires through which a voltage was applied, allowed scientists in the late nineteenth century to find the standing wave nodes or crossing points along the waves, and thus to measure the wavelength.[3, 4]

The Lecher line is a pair of parallel wires which join to form a loop at one end. It is used to tune in with the patterns formed as electromagnetic waves travel simultaneously along the parallel wires. Standing waves are induced by a resonant source, which emits electro-magnetic waves. As these standing waves form along the wires, the interference pattern

---

[3] Ernst Lecher and His Wires – Radio Science Bulletin No 369 June 2019 *Maddio and Selleri*, University of Florence. http://www.ursi.org/content/RSB/RSB_369_2019_06.pdf

[4] https://waveguide.blog/lecher-lines-translation-original-paper-ernst-lecher/ (May 2019)

enables both detection of the nodes, and measurement of the length of the waves. Varying the setting of the cross-bridge allows different wavelengths to be detected and lets us tune in with different stations along the loop or 'antenna'.

Ernst Lecher experimented using a gas filled glass tube across the wire ends, in place of a direct metal loop. In his experiments he created a short circuit by placing a metal crossbridge across the parallel wires between the source and the gas filled glass tube. By moving the shorting wire (crossbridge) along the loop he discovered that the gas in the tube would illuminate with the crossbridge at very distinct intervals along the loop. He discovered that shorting the wires at specific points along the loop, was a very accurate way to find the wave nodes and thus measure wavelength.[5]

Lecher was able to demonstrate that his system worked to illuminate the glass vial even if he cut the wires, effectively creating two separate circuits. Provided he had a short across the wires in both resonating circuits, the gas would illuminate. Using this apparatus, where the illuminated circuit appeared to be totally disconnected from the circuit with the resonating source, Lecher demonstrated that a direct connection is not required for the transmission of the waves along a Lecher loop.[6,7]

The Lecher antenna is an incredibly useful tool in the hands of ACMOS Bio-energetics practitioners, and practitioners in the fields of radiesthesia and geobiology. The Lecher loop is still used in experiments

---

[5] Frank Thompson, University of Manchester.
http://www.start-simply.co.uk/wp-content/uploads/2017/07/Lech_Lines_22_Sept.pdf

[6] https://www.vastuandmore.com/angebote-und-leistungen-lecher-antenne- und-schwingungsfrequenzen/

[7] In German language. Shows the original adaptation of Lechers lines into a Lecher antenna by Reinhard Schneider a German Professor of Physics. http://www.biosensor-physik.de/biosensor/grifflaenge.htm

in physics today[8], yet it's usage in vibrational medicine is still relatively unknown.

The Lecher loop was used to transmit and receive radio waves throughout the history of the twentieth century.

In early days you had to turn a knob which moved a slider (the crossbridge) along the face of the radio unit until it hit the station. Changing stations was a bit fiddley. Sometimes a very small adjustment (along the hidden Lecher loop) helped to re-tune into the radio station, and you could hear the music more clearly. Eventually the digital revolution surpassed the need for hand tuned devices, but the Lecher loop continues to serve as a re-calibration tool.

---

[8] https://docplayer.org/72077214-Ausstellung-ueber-reinhard-schneider-auf- dem-internationalen-radiaesthesie-kongress-schwingungswelten-2006- tradition-wissenschaft-methodik-und.html

# Chapter Three: An Introduction to Resonance

All energetic matters emit vibrations. Some of those vibrations are beneficial to us and some are not. This is infinitely variable between individuals dependent upon the interaction between their hereditary programming, the strength of their main energy channel and the circumstances which have affected them during their lives. Examples of energetic interactions include relationships with other people or animals, and both internal and external environments.

Quantum Physics has shown that at the subatomic level, matter is energy, and consists of energetic systems interacting with each other. All matter emits *subtle* energy or photons — particles of light. The Lecher Antenna is able to tune into and measure these subtle energy emissions.

The antenna is as much an emitter as it is a receiver. It acts in a similar way to an old-fashioned transistor radio both seeking and emitting when it is set on a specific wavelength. Sliding the crossbridge (shunt) changes the wavelength or signal detected and allows the antenna to tune into different signals in the environment around it, be they animal, vegetable or mineral.

Everything, around us and within us, vibrates in tune with the natural forces of the universe and of the Earth. By tuning into and strengthening these fundamental signals, the antenna may unblock the energy and restore VIBRATORY BALANCE. This can be thought of as restoring our natural vibrations to a harmonious state, by ensuring our connections are both tuned into and balanced with the grand energetic forces of life on Earth.

There is no question that the human body emits, receives and reacts to electromagnetic signals. The body emits light at the infrared part of the electromagnetic spectrum, which can be detected using night vision equipment, as used by the military to detect the heat signature from people hiding in the dark or buried by earthquakes. Excessive exposure to ultraviolet waves can burn and damage the skin.

Both the heart and brain generate powerful electromagnetic fields. The field of the human heart is as much as 60 times stronger than the field of the brain, and the heart field is measurable several feet away from the body. In 1998, the HeartMath Institute published a paper which demonstrated that when people are within close proximity, the electro-magnetic fields of their hearts interact with a transference of electromagnetic energy. *The Electricity of Touch: Detection and Measurement of Cardiac Energy Exchange Between People, McCraty, Atkinson et al.*

Most people are unaware of waves in the suprasensible part of the electromagnetic spectrum, the signals which we cannot interpret using the five main senses. These waves entangle or interact with the human body creating resonance. All lifeforms tune into these imperceptible signals in the environment.

An Antenna is simply a useful tool, to tune into the world of resonance and to assess the electro-magnetic effect of entanglement between living things and their environment. Application of Lecher's physics gives a numerical reference point, on a centimetre scale, at the wave nodes along the Lecher loop of the antenna. Knowing the numbers allows us to interpret aspects of this interactive, vibratory information.

# Chapter Four:
# The ACMOS Lecher Antenna

The Lecher antenna was created in the 1950s by German Physicist Reinhardt Schneider as a modification of the Lecher loop. Schneider based his antenna on the same principle of resonance along parallel wires. He used the antenna in radiesthesia as a more scientific application of dowsing. Subsequently the Lecher Antenna was applied by radiesthesia and Feng Shui practitioners to detect radiation emitted by people, animals, objects and to assess the environment for example to find areas of geopathic stress.

Meanwhile in Paris, energy medicine researcher, Dr René Naccachian PhD had been using electronic biofeedback, to assess and monitor change in the meridian circuits of his patients, since the 1970s. Dr Naccachian, who began his career as an instrumentation engineer, had gained doctorates in energy medicine and in molecular biology after a personal encounter with Chinese medicine changed his life. His life's work then became the development of innovative products and systems to balance energy. For years he honed the implementation and analysis of his ACMOS Method, improving the health of his family, friends, and many other people.

Early in the 1990s, a Feng Shui practitioner came to analyse Dr Naccachian's home using a Lecher antenna. Excited to find a tool to measure resonance without having to have direct contact, Dr Naccachian applied his knowledge of engineering and physics, to adapt the antenna to pick up subtle information from the human body. The Lecher antenna gave him the inspiration to test out the instrument, as a way to measure how the energetic quality of objects and spaces affected people, by noting changes in their bio-fields.

A lifelong thirst for knowledge, and the urge to understand the effects of objects and remedies on his clients, led Dr Naccachian to develop antenna techniques which enhanced or reduced the energetic impact of all aspects of life, on the person, thereby strengthening their bio-fields.

The aim of this book is to start or complement your journey into the wonderful world of resonance and the possibilities this knowledge brings to resonant health. By adapting the use of the Lecher device, to measure the energy fields surrounding the human body, and to analyse the effect of objects on the person's energy fields, the ACMOS Method of today was born.

The ACMOS Lecher Antenna is now the most essential tool of the ACMOS practitioner, who uses it to:

- Measure the vibrations of energy signals and fields.

- Transfer information and strengthen signals.

- Evaluate the outcome of any interventions.

The vibrational phenomenon, of like tunes in with like, allows us to study the quality of the environment, and its effect on the individuals and groups who live within it. The Lecher antenna is used around the globe in health and geobiology.

The Lecher antenna is a sensitive sender and receiver of signals in the UHF and VHF part of the electromagnetic spectrum. The wavelengths that it picks up are measured in nanometres however, a centimetre scale was adopted early in the antenna's history as it is an easy to see, reproducible scale which is simple to use.

*Dr Naccachian called the units of scale on his antenna **ACTU** for ACMOS Cosmo-Telluric Units.*

The ACTU measuring scale has been placed inside the Lecher loop and is highlighted by a small mark at the most important wavelengths. These numbers become familiar as the language of the antenna as they are used regularly in day-to-day practise. Knowing the meaning of the numbers allows you to interpret your findings.

Light energy or electromagnetic energy travels along the wires of the antenna and where there is resonance the antenna moves or dips in the hands of the operator. The meaning of any observation is dependent upon the setting of the crossbridge at various stations along the antenna.

This simple principle means that when a matching or resonant signal is encountered as you scan over a person or an item, the antenna moves, and you feel it slide within your grip. When a wavelength is not detected this means the signal is too faint to create sufficient resonance to move the antenna.

Whilst the ACMOS Method is a complete system of energetic tuning or 'balancing', the antenna alone has a variety of uses. The ACMOS antenna with its sliding scale, and crossbridge allows users to tune into a wide range of wavelengths, allowing them to:

- Measure their own energy fields.

- Measure the energy fields of others.

- Measure the energetic quality of foods, supplements, jewellery, buildings and assess their interactions.

**Note:** The signals we test occur naturally all around us, we must therefore ensure that we focus on the test object or person, or we may inadvertently pick up a nearby signal.

The ACMOS Lecher Antenna (ALA) can also be used to:

- Personalise the use of supplements and remedies.

- Assist global balance by identifying at which level the human energy system has lost its resonance.

- Restore the missing signal where appropriate.

The following steps will teach you how to strengthen a weak signal, in an object, a space or a person, to bring a faint signal up to the quality of the signal emitted by the antenna.

The antenna sends the correct wave signal to open the energetic quality of a room or space, the human energy drivers and thus the main human energy channel.

After a period of practical application, you will be able to use the antenna to check the compatibility of any products, which are used within the energy fields, to ensure that they work harmoniously with the person using them.

When we restore a missing vibration, we improve the resonance and enhance the vibratory (or vibrating) quality of the products we use in our daily lives – our mobile phones, the colours and jewellery we wear, the cosmetics we use, the supplements we take, the foods we eat.

Our environment is increasingly cluttered with white noise or signals. Just think of every phone or television station on the planet emitting their own unique bandwidths and wave signals.

Add to that the signals from satellites that we tune into without thinking whenever we access electronic maps.

Gadgets have transformed our lives bringing both benefits and additional stress on our inbuilt, human, signalling and super-sensory communication systems.

Improving our energetic resilience, the core strength of the energy body, increases our ability to cope with the myriad of vibrating signals in today's busy environment.

Once you have a positive response from the antenna to the questions on the following page, you can start to make healthy changes, to improve your own energetic strength, you can improve the energetic quality of your home, your workplace and, with their permission you can start to optimise resilience in your family and friends.

# IMPORTANT

## BEFORE WE BEGIN

Good practice requires you to respect the inherent wisdom of the energy body. Ask for permission prior to making *any* changes in anyone's personal energy with your antenna.

- **Can I open this signal** (or connection) for this person/ object? You will often get a positive response to 'can I' but to 'do so' may not be in the best interest of the recipient.

- **May I open this signal** for this person/ object? A respectful request for permission from the energy body you are working with – ask when resetting your own energy too.

- **Should I open this signal** for this person/ object? Is the change you intend to make in the best interests of the person? This is a *very* important question.

- **Do I have the capacity to make this change?** You do not want to drain your own energy reserves.

# Chapter Five:
# Getting Started with Your Antenna

## Store the Antenna in the folded position

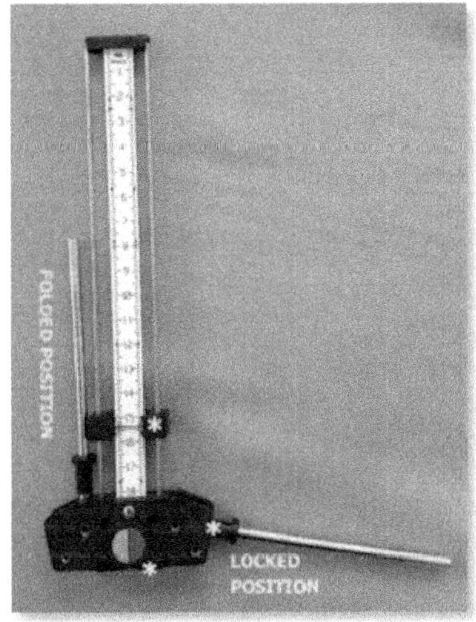



The antenna is a tool for measuring the presence of vibrational signals.

It tunes in with specific wavelengths, emitting AND receiving signals especially once the arms are opened. The antenna broadcasts the wavelength, set on the sliding scale.

New antennas can feel a little stiff, but the moving parts* relax or loosen slightly with use.

*Gently* introduce the locking pegs, into the black base unit of the antenna, to fix the handles in place. Over time the block will loosen slightly, and it will be easier to insert the pegs.

*If you force the pegs into the block this may damage your antenna.*

When folding up the antenna make sure that the locking pegs are held between the sliding cross-bridge and the black base of the antenna. The pegs loosen over time, slide more easily, and can slip off. You will not lose the pegs if you store your antenna in this way.

Using an antenna requires time and practise to become proficient – the more that you learn and understand the better and more accurate your results will be.

Unfold the arms of the antenna, and gently push the stabilising plugs into the black base of the antenna. These should fit snugly to hold the antenna firmly in the open position, however, if they are forced in too tightly then over time, they can become loose.

Always refold the antenna with the cross-bridge or 'curser' above the 2 black plugs. The curser acts as a block to prevent the plugs sliding off the arms when the antenna is not in use.

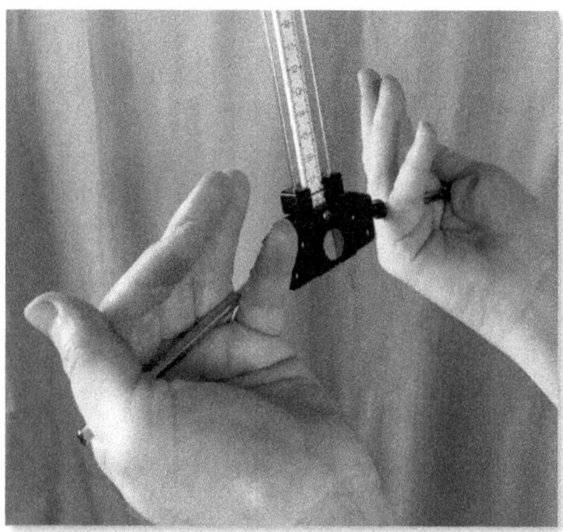

Hold the opened antenna between your 4th and 5th fingers with the numbers facing you. The metal handles sit behind your little finger and in front of the middle 3 fingers.

Stabilise the antenna by placing your thumbs in front of the free ends of the metal handles.

Hold the antenna tightly enough so that it does not slip or swivel due to gravity alone. Do not hold it so tightly that it cannot move but you can hold it firmly.

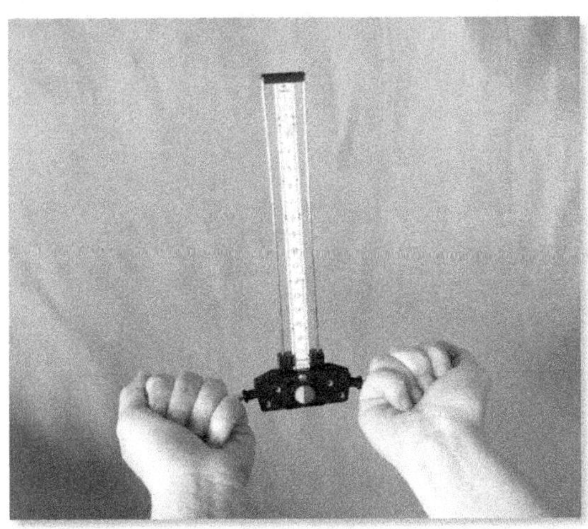

When starting hold the antenna with your elbows straight. If you find your antenna moves for everything, tighten your grip. If it never appears to move relax your grip. As you become more proficient you can relax your arms at the elbow.

Over time this will start to feel completely natural as you and your antenna become more in tune. It is very important to keep your thoughts clear, to focus on the task you are completing and to ensure of any intention is absolutely pure.

It is easier to start in a position where gravity assists you. It is therefore standard practise to have the top of the wire loop tipped slightly towards you as your starting position. If the antenna leans away from you, it will have to overcome gravity, and create inertia in order to move when it resonates, with any item that you are testing.

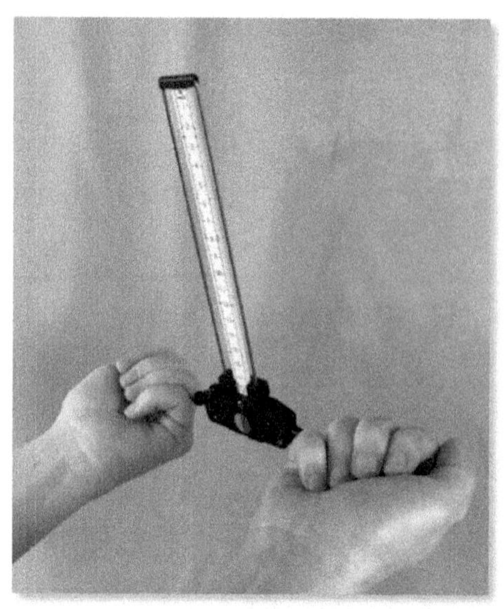

## TOP TIP

To feel the sensation of the antenna twisting between your fingers, ask a friend to help you by pushing the tip towards you.

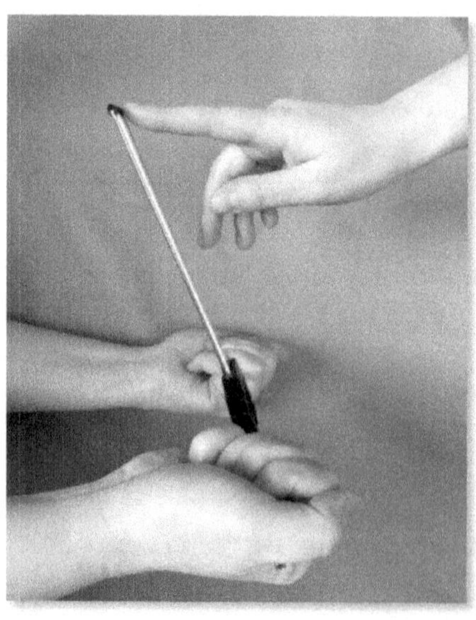

Close your eyes, hold as tightly as you can and then ask them to push without telling you when. Can you sense and feel the antenna move?

At the base of the antenna, you will see 2 small holes.

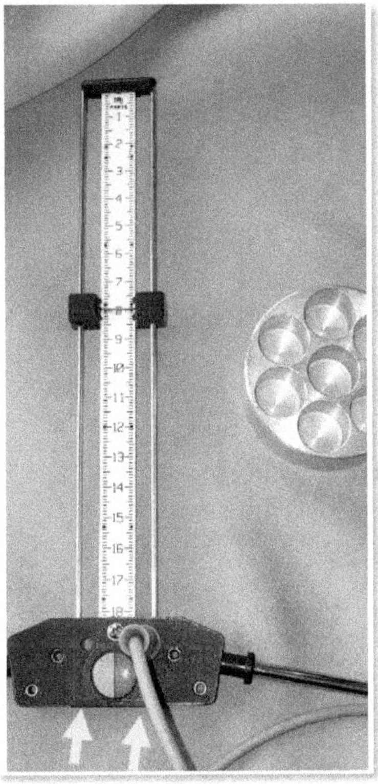

These holes are in line with the wire of the Lecher loop.

Information, in the form of wave signals, is broad- cast or received through these small holes — make sure that these are pointed *directly* towards the item or person you are measuring.

The cable connects via the *right* hole as in the picture.

# Chapter Six:
# Exercises to Help You Connect



## Preparation

1.  Try to be in the moment, outside of your thinking brain. Take 2 or 3 deep breaths allowing the breath to reach the sacral energy centre (below your tummy button). Concentrate on the breath out and on feeling the floor beneath your feet. **Be** in the moment.

2.  There is no right and wrong, there is only what **is**. Let go of the fear of getting it wrong. That is why you practise.

3.  You are learning a new sense, so try to listen to or tune into the feelings in your body and your hands, as you operate the antenna. This sense of position and movement in space is called proprioception. You will become accustomed to the sensation of how *your* antenna moves in your grip, when it picks up a resonance.

4.  Be patient with yourself and *feel* from a sense of non- judgemental detachment. Widen your knowledge of energy medicine and the physics of resonance, so that you can understand what you are feeling. Learning should be fun as a whole new world of information opens up, quite literally at your fingertips.

5.  Choose a quiet place to practise, away from phones, TVs, other people. It is easier to concentrate if there are no distractions.

6.  Avoid practising after eating while your energy is busy with the process of digestion, and you may feel lethargic.

7.  Finish each session with the 2-3 deeps breaths centring yourself
    once again in the moment, in mindful meditation.

## EXERCISES TO SENSE & CONNECT WITH THE ALA

1.  Figures of 8: hold the antenna firmly with **one** hand. Make
    sweeping figures of eight in the air, feel as the antenna wants to
    slide in your hand but hold it firmly. Practise 6 times with one
    hand with then repeat with the other hand. Remember to breathe
    and be in the moment.

2.  Hold the open antenna in one hand by your side, then swing it
    diagonally upwards across your body towards your opposite
    shoulder by bending your elbow. Keep the antenna upright even
    though you will sense it wants to move. Return to the starting
    position and repeat for least 6 times. Breathe then repeat with
    your other hand. Rest if your arm feels tired as this will interfere
    with your sense of connection with the antenna.

3.  Use both hands to grip the antenna, palms up, antenna tipped
    slightly towards you, numbers facing you. Grip the handles very
    tightly and ask someone to push the tip of the antenna towards
    you. Try to resist. You will feel the antenna rotate between your
    $4^{th}$ and $5^{th}$ fingers. This is the sensation that you will feel when
    testing. Close your eyes and repeat this until it becomes a felt
    sense.

4.  Grip the antenna as in 3 above. Allow the antenna to drop or slide
    forwards about 30 degrees, then flick it up to restore it to the
    starting position. This exercise allows you to find a rhythm with
    your antenna. The aim is to teach your hands to instinctively react
    to the antenna's movement, it is not an exercise in testing.

*Note*: When you are testing make sure to hold the antenna more firmly than when you are doing this exercise.

## HANDY TIPS

Hold the antenna gently but firmly with the top of the antenna tipped slightly towards you as you scan over objects. As it moves (in response to a resonance) you will feel the antenna slide round between your fingers. Reset it to the starting position for the next scan.

*Do not check your response over and over.*
*Practice so that you learn to trust*
*your **first** response.*

The antenna emits as well as receives the signal you are looking for. If the object is exposed repeatedly to the same wavelength emitted by the antenna (i.e., whichever number you have set on the centimetre scale with the cross-bridge shunt) this exposure can raise the vibration of the object to that wavelength. Repeated testing may bring the object you are checking into resonance and give a false positive.

Although most people find it easier to scan with your elbows almost straight to start with, once you can feel the resonance you can relax your arms more.

Hold the antenna relatively tightly:

- If everything you scan responds, tighten your grip so that you are sure that the antenna is sliding rather than falling in your grip.

- If nothing responds loosen your grip and practice the warm-up breathing exercise to be more focused in the moment.

- If you get frustrated take a break as you are no longer in the moment.

Learn to be precise when taking measurements. Once you learn about the numbers on the antenna you will realise that these are natures numbers. These are naturally emitted signals, and they are all around us all the time.

There is a simple technique which helps focus your attention on the target area.

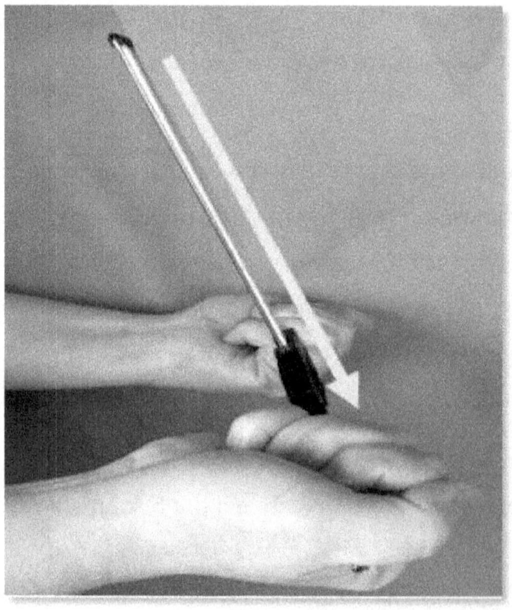

Hold the antenna gently in your hands with the top of the loop towards you. Look along the length of the antenna as if it were a crossbow. The scale of the antenna is 20 cm long – with your eye at 0 cm at the top of the scale, look down the length of the antenna. Visualise the 2 holes at the base of the antenna at the 20th centimetre training onto your 'target'.

Is the target area in your line of sight?

Using the targeting technique, measure lots of different objects until you feel at ease with the response that you have with your antenna. Everyone's response is personal to them, and the loop does not have to move very far, as long as you feel the response.

When you measure *yourself,* aim at your 'reflection' on a flat white or neutral surface. We take a reflected reading off a plain wall as it is difficult to direct the beams of the antenna towards yourself. This step is covered in detail in Chapter nine.

# CHAPTER SEVEN: WAVELENGTHS ON THE ANTENNA

The most significant wavelengths are selected by moving the cross-bridge on the Lecher loop as follows:

**2.1**    VITALITY of the lymphatic system

**2.5**    HARMONIOUS with the human cell wavelength

**8**    SEDATING, calming — YIN

**12**    EXCITING, stimulating — YANG

**15.3**    RADIATING, combination of yin and yang, 'balanced' dynamic energy

**17.6**    REGENERATING, 'intelligent' dynamic energy which also enhances elimination

**17.6**    is used for ALL QUESTIONING and to check if items add to the energetic quality (harmonious) or have a detrimental effect

*Note*: The ACMOS training material is colour coded to correspond to the features above. **17.6** is pink to reflect the fact that it aids elimination and therefore, although it carries a high vibration, it is more yang than yin in nature.

## The Vital 'Driving' Forces (Energy Drivers)

The most important settings on the antenna for the beginner to understand are **8** and **12**. These are the energetic driving forces which apply to all aspects of life on Earth – the interaction of the tensions of our local universe on our bodies, our pets, our homes, and our wider environment. The Earth is precisely located at the 'correct' distance from the sun to allow life here to flourish. We are also influenced by the Earth's relationship with the moon and the other planets.

**TELLURIC DRIVER** = 8 ACTU* is the resonance through which we connect with the centripetal or calming force of the energy of the EARTH. Over the past century, we have insulated ourselves from this calming influence by placing man-made material on the soles of our shoes. If someone frequently loses their earth or TELLURIC connection, measured at **8** on the antenna scale, you could suggest they walk barefoot on grass or on the earth. Activities should be calming in nature e.g., meditation, yoga, **YIN.**

**COSMIC DRIVER** = 12 ACTU* is the resonance through which we connect with the radiant or centrifugal energy of the SUN and the COSMOS. Often we live our lives indoors and do not spend enough time outdoors. If someone frequently loses their COSMIC or solar connection, measured at **12** on the antenna scale, suggest that they spend more time outside. Activities should be active and outgoing in nature e.g., a dynamic sport, **YANG.**

**COSMO-TELLURIC CHANNEL** = 15.3 ACTU* is the balanced tension of the **8** and the **12**. When these two driving forces are in harmony with each other the **15.3** will resonate.

> *ACTU = ACMOS Cosmo-Telluric Units The units of the scale on the antenna (cosmic = from the cosmos/sun; telluric = from the earth).

In humans we measure 15.3 at the centre of the chest. When there is resonance (the antenna dips), there is synergy and balance in the Cosmo-

Telluric Channel. The vital forces of the cosmos and the earth are finely tuned and resonate well with the person being tested.

Deficiencies in these natural tensions can be easily rectified with an antenna, however, it is important to recognise that living organisms use their interaction with these essential life forces to manage their energy systems.

## The Third Driving Force

There is a third vital driving force, connecting us with the centre-point around which the universe turns, our spiritual connection point with all that is, and our 'connectedness' with the rest of humanity.

Like the telluric driver, the 1.1 is centripetal or **YIN** in nature. The third driver connects us by intaking force through the centre of the earth, with the central force of our solar system, our sun and then through the centre of the sun to the centre of our galaxy, and thus to our position in the universe.

We do not adjust this connection directly.

This connection with source, and with our energetic blueprint is blocked by the energy body when it perceives a significant threat. It will only re-establish coherence or re-open once the underlying cause has been resolved.

Once the energy body is connected to the primary drivers of 8 and 12, sufficiently well to restore the 15.3 Cosmo-Telluric channel, and to restore elimination functions at 17.6, the energy body will often restore the third driver without further intervention. This important connection with source is discussed in great detail during the ACMOS Method training seminars.

The three drivers are the cornerstones of this transformational Method of balancing deeply hidden blocks in the energy body and its systems.

We therefore treat the drivers with the upmost respect.

# Chapter Eight: Measure Rooms & Spaces

Always start every session by assessing the energetic quality of the space you are working in. It is essential to make sure that the energy of the space is open and resonates well before doing any further testing.

Focus your intention very clearly on the information you seek

If the space is unbalanced, this will affect the work you do within that space, as it affects your energy, and that of your test case. Begin by scanning the corners to confirm the presence of the two, most basic, vital energy drivers. Then scan to confirm that these forces are in balance at the centre of the room.

METHOD Check the *energy drivers* at the four corners of the room with the antenna set on:

**8** scan the lower or *floor corners* to check the earth or yin connection of the space – does the antenna move?

**12** scan at the upper or *ceiling corners* to check the yang or cosmic connection of the space – does the antenna move?

Remember the targeting exercise as you aim for the corners. Sweep the antenna gently across from your left side and fix your line of sight on the corner of the room as precisely as you can. Wait a moment or two for the antenna to dip but do not remain there if there is no response. Note your results.

*Trust your first reading as repeated testing may*
*open a weak area and confuse you with a false*
*positive result.*

If the corners of the room appear open, set the curser on **15.3** and scan across the centre of the room or space using the antenna. Stop in the centre of the space and wait a moment or two for the antenna to dip which confirms the Cosmo-Telluric channel of the space.

If either the **8** or the **12** is sluggish or blocked
**15.3** should NOT resonate in the
centre of the room.

Start the scan with the base of the antenna pointing away from the centre of the room so that, when you stop in the middle of the space, you can feel whether the vibration changes and notice if the antenna moves. It is helpful to have your arms straight when you are learning.

## Is The Movement Absent?

If the **15.3** is absent, the room has a weak connection with either the earth **8** or the cosmic energy **12**. Does one *driver* respond more strongly than the other?

*Remember* **15.3** is the point on the antenna scale which resonates when the forces of the earth driver **8** and the cosmic driver **12** are in a *balanced* state of tension — whether you are assessing a space, a room, an object, or a person.

Once you have discovered where there is a block in the energy of the room, you can re-activate the missing signal with the antenna (see Chapter eleven) — you can impose the weak energy driver to open the space.

## VIBRATORY TOXINS – Spent Energy

In ACMOS, we understand that old light or vibratory toxins are continuously being eliminated from the body, so that these vibratory toxins do not accumulate in our vulnerable areas. When this spent energy leaves the body*, it can gather in a confined space causing stagnation – when this happens the **17.6** of the room becomes blocked.

If the room is energetically blocked (8 or 12 is weak causing the 15.3 to be lost) this old energy will already be polluting the space we inhabit, and the room will have lost its 17.6.

*There are many means to eliminate matter from the body. It is as important to clean the spent energy from our systems, as it is to get rid of old matter, which no longer gives us any benefit.

Check the centre of the space on **17.6** to see whether (a) the energy is moving and (b) any vibratory toxins are clearing adequately from the area. The space can block before a driver goes off, so the 17.6 of the room will only be present when ALL the other readings are open.

If the **17.6** does *not* respond, go back to the weakest driver (8 or 12). Make sure that the drivers are strong, and if the 17.6 still does not open, ventilate the area by opening a window or moving the furniture to create more space. Re- check the area on **17.6.**

Force creates movement – it causes energy to move – to flow. By tuning into the forces of the cosmos and the earth, we ensure that the energetic quality of any space is as stable as possible.

POINT OF PRINCIPLE – each step in the energetic hierarchy affects the others. We therefore start with the basics – the vital driving forces. Without movement of the energy, the effect of vibratory toxins is magnified.

# Chapter Nine: Measure Your Own Energy

Having checked the room, it is essential to check yourself before trying to balance others, or even to take accurate readings from objects, nutritional supplements, foods etc.

If *your* Cosmo-Telluric channel is blocked your results will be inconsistent.

We follow a very similar process to checking the room, except this time we check that you are connected to the vital driving forces (8 & 12), that these forces are in balance (15.3) and that you are clearing your vibratory toxins efficiently (17.6).

When using the Lecher antenna to measure yourself, slide out the drawer at the base of the antenna to remove the insulation between your hands and the loop of wire, which connects with the sliding shunt.

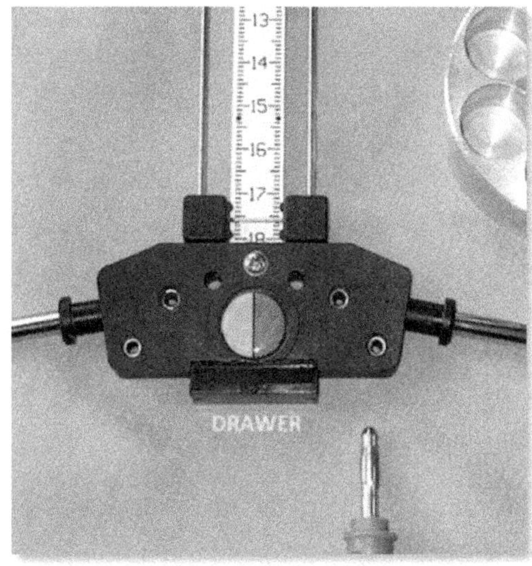


*Opening the drawer is easier with the arms folded.*

You now have a more energetic connection with the antenna.

*Note*: For all other uses make sure the drawer is pushed into the closed position, this is to insulate your energy from the object, room or individual you are measuring.

## OPEN THE DRAWER AT THE BASE OF THE ANTENNA

Face a blank wall, preferably neutral or white, to capture your energetic *reflection* as it rebounds from the wall — do not use a mirror.

Set the antenna at:

- **12** — check your cosmic connection by scanning in from the left side, target the base of the antenna at the wall opposite the top of your head.

  If the antenna dips in your hands there is resonance, your cosmic connection resonates (we say your **12** is open or on).

- **8** — check your earth connection by sca nning in from the side as above, focusing the holes at the base of the antenna *below* the centre of your pelvis. If there is resonance the antenna responds by moving — your earth connection is open (or your **8** is on).

- **15.3** — scan the wall level with the centre of the chest to check that your Cosmo-Telluric channel* (CT- also called the human main energy channel) is open and resonating well with the antenna. (15.3 is on)

- **17.6** – scan the wall at the centre of the chest to check that your global vibratory energy** is balanced *and* that you are able to clear your vibratory toxins efficiently.

*Remember*: The Cosmo-Telluric channel is measured at **15.3** at the chest. It is the 'sum of' the balanced tension between the cosmic force (**12**) and the earth force (**8**).

*Note:* **17.6** at the chest is the combined sum of all three grand driving forces (8, 12 and 1.1), therefore in the ACMOS Method we refer to 17.6 at the chest as the **GLOBAL VIBRATORY BALANCE. *Any* major loss of resonance at any of the other measurements upsets the whole, the 'global'.

Look along the metal loop of the antenna like a crossbow and aim for the target area – in this case above the head to measure your own **12**.

# Chapter Ten:
# Measure Objects & Foods

**Always check** that *your* Cosmo-Telluric channel is open before testing objects and other people.**15.3** at the chest.

Selecting objects to measure is important when looking to gain confidence with your antenna. Objects made or chosen with love tend to carry a higher vibration, and therefore make better, or rather easier, test objects.

Compare this type of object with something toxic such as bleach or other harmful chemicals to get a real feel for the difference between a positive and a missing response.

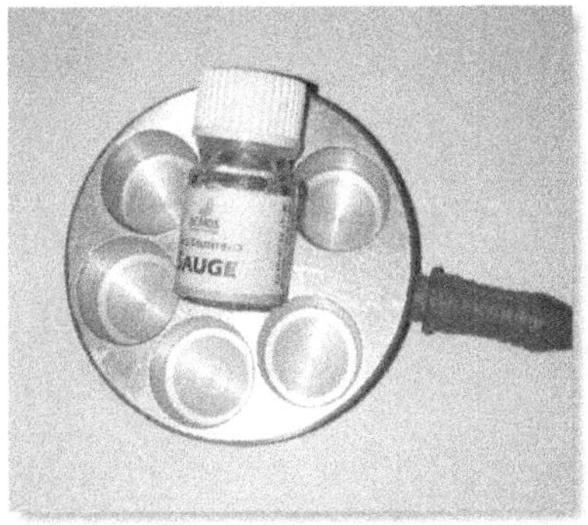

Connect the antenna to the mass using the cable. Place the object on the metal mass on a neutral surface. Set the cross-bridge at **2.5** and scan across the object e.g., jewellery from left to right stopping directly over the object. Wait a second or two.

Does the antenna respond? I.e., does it tune into the vibration of the object and move downwards in your hands?

Start the scan with the base of the antenna pointing away from the object so that you can feel whether the vibration changes when you scan the antenna over the object.

If the antenna moves, the object has the minimum **2.5** ACTU wavelength needed to be harmonious with the human body.

After obtaining a response at **2.5** ACTU move the cursor to **17.6**, to see if the object you are measuring also has regenerating or therapeutic properties.

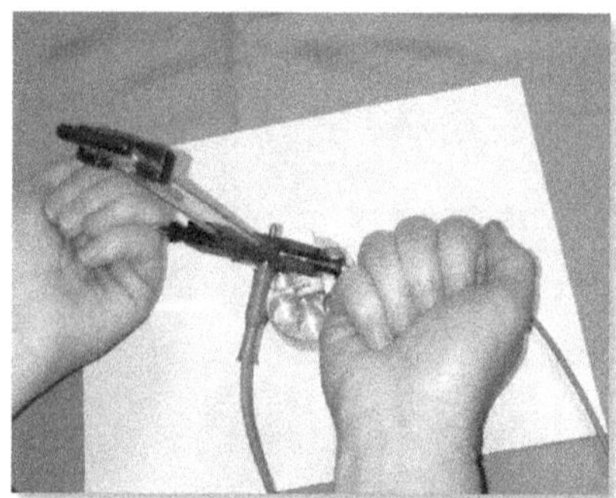

***Note:*** If the antenna does not respond to **2.5**, the object is incompatible which means it will take more energy from the body than it gives. To energetically clean the object, or activate the energy by imposing, see Chapter eleven.

Incompatible objects can cause the body to react and may create an energetic block as a self-defence mechanism.

The language of the antenna — the numbers, remain the same no matter what we are assessing. However, our understanding changes, as we consider each situation.

Are the *energetic* forces are affecting either; an object? Or a person? Is the space influencing the reading?

Is the space affecting the person? Is an object affecting the person? Or is the person inherently fragile?

## How to Measure Foods and Nutritional Supplements

Repeat the same process shown earlier to measure the vibrational quality of foods and supplements. A useful table to help with Product Analysis is in appendix one.

Experiment with a wide variety of foods in varying states of freshness. Fruits, especially berries, carry a high vibration and if you have oranges or capsicum where one part has deteriorated, then test a group and see if you can pick out the fruit which is past its best. It is very handy to be able to test items in your refrigerator to see whether they are still compatible with humans.

If something responds at **2.5** it carries the minimum resonance acceptable to humans so, although it is not ideal, it is still edible. If it resonates at **8** it is calming, as an example, a herbal tea before bed should resonate at 8. Items which respond at **12** are stimulating, such as a coffee to wake up in the morning.

Foods which resonate at **15.3** are radiantly healthy and will contribute more energy to your body. 15.3 products support the balance of your Cosmo-Telluric energy.

Items which resonate at **17.6** have greater vitality and add to your energetic quality. In addition to balance they facilitate regeneration.

## Technique

Move the antenna in from the left, scan over the item on **2.5** to assess whether the food, nutrient or supplement has this minimum energetic quality. Repeat the process with the antenna set on **17.6** to see whether the product is regenerating. A product with **17.6** will be more beneficial as it assists the body's elimination capacities, as well as providing dynamic radiating energy.

# Chapter Eleven:
# Activate Energy in Objects

When the energy in the space is not moving it has become stagnant due to a weak driver or a cluttered space. The technique we use to open a blocked driver is called IMPOSING.

We use imposing to strengthen the energetic connection of a room or in objects, foods, supplements, etc.

Move the base of the antenna:

- Down over the object or area,

- Across over the object or area to make the *plus sign +*,

- Wait over the centre of the object or space until the antenna moves or dips in your hands.

This + pulls the cosmic energy down and the movement across locks it in. The wait allows time for the natural forces to tune in and reassert themselves – they are always there!

IMPOSING A ROOM — decide which vital driving force is weaker and strengthen the weakest area of the room first:

- Identify the weakest corner of the room at floor level with the cross-bridge set at 8 ACTU. If there is no resonance or only a weak dip, impose with the antenna to strengthen the Earth connection (plus sign on 8),

- Identify the weakest corner of the room at ceiling level with the cross-bridge set at 12 ACTU. If there is no resonance or only a weak dip, impose with the antenna to strengthen the Cosmic connection of the room (plus sign on 12),

- Check to see if the energy of the room is restored by re- checking the centre of the room at 15.3.

Where an object or nutrient does not respond to **2.5** you can activate the energy by making a plus sign over the object with the antenna.

## Imposing An Object

Place the object on top of the metal mass on a neutral surface. The cable should connect the antenna with the object.

Set **2.5** ACTU on the antenna using the cross-bridge. Scan from left to right – if there is no response to 2.5 make the plus sign with the antenna to impose or open the energy flow.

The + pulls down the cosmic energy and locks it in. Scan the item again from left to right to check if the object or space has maintained the **2.5** vibration which you have strengthened.

You can repeat this process on **17.6** to improve the energetic quality of the object. If necessary repeat the process.

*Note:* I prefer to ask which wavelength works most harmoniously with the energy of the person. When imposing a product or object I therefore offer the range of 2.5, 8, 12, 15.3 and 17.6 as options when asking whether I can improve the quality of that object for that person.

Over time you will learn that there are differences in the response for different people. A strong indication that a one- size approach does not work best to optimise vibrational health.

## Appendix four – the antenna protocol

Column one, change the vibration of a product, gives you a simple way to access the right setting to use. Always question to find the best solution at that point in time.

# Chapter Twelve: Measure Other People

You should always make sure your own Cosmo-Telluric channel is open before working on anyone else. If your channel is blocked, you will not be able to assess the energy fields of your subject accurately.

You are becoming familiar with the different settings on the antenna, and you can now apply these same measurements to find out what is happening to another person's energy.

## First check yourself (Chapter Nine)

If your energy channel is blocked you will not be able to accurately assess the energy of your test case. Your vibrational dissonance may tune in with and upset their energy.

If you have no tension on **15.3** at your chest, find your weak or absent driver (**8** or **12**) and ask if you can re-activate it by imposing, using the plus sign.

After confirming your channel is open, ask the person you are testing to hold the metal mass, with the cable plugged into it, in their *dominant hand*. Plug the other end of the cable into the *right hole* as you face your antenna.

The dominant hand transmits information; we communicate in writing and by gesticulating with the dominant hand. We use this naturally radiating communication, to access the energetic information with the antenna.

Scanning in from the left side when measuring, gives the antenna impetus and allows it to move more easily over the 'test' area. Whenever a wavelength is not detected, this means that the signal is too faint to create a standing wave in the antenna circuit. There is little or no resonance. We will discover what you can do to open the energy later.

Face your test case with the intention only to measure:

- Check the cosmic connection above the head at **12** ACTU. If 12 is absent: **Ask** if it can be reconnected by imposing. If not, it must be re-opened by following the antenna protocol or by a strict ACMOS protocol.

- Check the earth connection between the feet at **8** ACTU. If it is absent: **Ask** if it can be reconnected by imposing. If not, it must be re-opened by following the antenna protocol or by a strict ACMOS protocol.

- Check the **15.3** ACTU at chest level confirming the presence of both channels: if absent; either the **8** ACTU or **12** ACTU is weak or missing. Ask — can I, may I, should I impose the weaker DRIVER?

The vibratory field or aura of the individual is measured with the antenna set at **2.5** ACTU at the *five main energy centres* or chakras: the forehead, throat, heart, solar plexus, and lower abdomen (hara).

- Check the five energy centres on **2.5** to understand the area of the block. If one or more areas are blocked review your findings. Was one driver weaker than the other?

- Ask — can I, may I, should I impose *the weaker driver* at the head **12** or feet **8**? Recheck the blocked 2.5 centre.

Finally we check for vibratory toxins, the old energy or LIGHT which is eliminated at the end of the cell's lifespan – a waste product of cellular renewal.

- Check the **17.6** ACTU at chest level. If the antenna dips this confirms the capacity of the energy body to eliminate its vibratory toxins.

In order to regenerate the body, old and dying cells are replaced with energetically vibrant new cells. These old cells have to be recycled or eliminated to prevent back-logs of debris forming in the body, which in ACMOS we call CELLULAR TOXINS.

The body does not recognise or eliminate cells which still contain energy. These old cells, which cannot eliminate their light component or VIBRATORY TOXINS, become blocked.

ACMOS theory suggests that most symptoms are the end result of old cells which have failed to be eliminated.

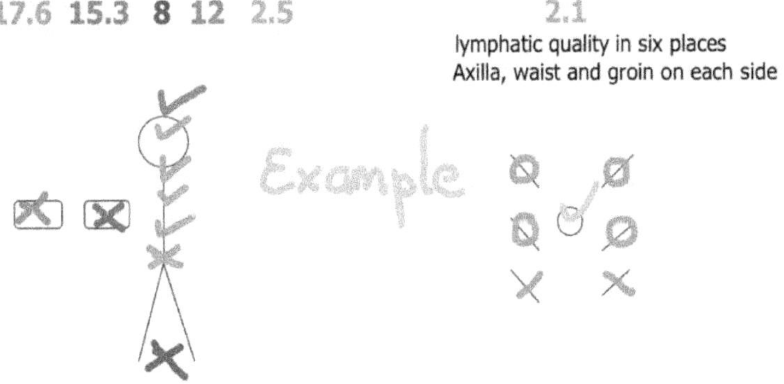



*Note:* Whilst it is possible to test **15.3** or **17.6** at the chest first, *this is a short cut* for those who *really* understand the energetic drivers, and how these influence our energy.

If the person loses the 17.6 at the chest, they are unable to eliminate their vibratory toxins quickly enough to keep up with the normal cellular regeneration work of the body. Eventually this backlog of blocked cells becomes a matter problem.

Wherever the **2.5** resonance is weak or absent, this suggests an energy block at a major energy centre. If the weakness is in the upper body, this may indicate a lack of cosmic connection just as a block in the lower part of the body may indicate a lack of earth connection.

*Note:* A blocked **2.5** will often open when you strengthen or impose the weaker driver — at the crown **12** or base **8**. If not, an energy balance is required.

In the ACMOS Method we **do not** impose the **2.5** to 'open the chakra'. We consider the chakras to be very important energy centres. The major chakras are points where the energy enters and exits the body. These are very important points for managing the areas under their influence.

In the ACMOS Method we refer to these important points as the regional managers, where the major endocrine glands, the physical body, meet the major energy centres of the energy body. These centres usually block for a reason related to self- management of the whole, and therefore should be allowed to open naturally when the cause of the block has been resolved.

2.5 is the synergy or balance of the driving forces 8 and 12
at the level of the main energy centres / chakras

All healthy cells transmit their vibratory field at 2.5

The exception to the **2.5** rule is an area of pain or scarring. In this case, if the area has lost its **2.5** resonance, restoring this connection with the 2.5 can balance the drivers to restore energy flow, and the area can then re-calibrate itself more efficiently.

Process: mentally divide the area into a grid and test across the whole area for blocks in the 2.5 As you scan the painful area with the antenna set on 2.5 there is no movement. Ask if you can, may and should open the energy directly to facilitate healing? If you are granted energetic permission then impose each area with the antenna set on 2.5 (+ sign)

There is a short protocol at the back of this book to guide you in asking the right questions and giving various options. Always follow the energetic intelligence.

## Elimination

Every day we replace billions of old cells in a natural, ongoing process. Our body has to eliminate both the energetic and the matter aspect of these old cells. Residual energy is eliminated into our environment as light and the cell structure or matter is ingested, broken down and recycled, or eliminated, via the lymphatic system (and allied specialised cells).

There are many routes of elimination from the body, however if the lymphatic system becomes blocked with old debris, then the efficiency of the other routes is eventually affected and there is stagnation in the body. The most efficient elimination route is via the urine however we all have our own natural tendencies.

Elimination routes: via the liver as bile, the kidneys as urine, the colon, the sweat, the tears, the skin…

Organic elimination refers to the energetic efficiency of these processes which begin with the clearing of cellular debris.

- Check organic elimination blocks* (lymphatic) at **2.1** ACTU at the armpits, lower ribs, and groin on both sides of the body where there are clusters of lymph nodes.

*The lymphatic system is highly energetic. When it functions well our bodies look after themselves much more efficiently. Old debris is cleared, immunity is more efficient and our radiance or whole of health is improved. We therefore measure the lymphatics early on in our testing and reactivate the lymphatic energy if it is blocked.

# Chapter Thirteen:
## Activate Energy in People

Imposing is also used to strengthen the energetic connection in people: This process activates their energy by reconnecting one of the drivers.

Managing the energetic connections is very subtle but deep work. Due respect should be accorded to the wisdom of the energy body, in electing to block what it perceives as destabilising signals. We do not assume that energy flow must be restored at all costs.

For this reason, you can only strengthen a weak wavelength or signal by imposing **IF** the energy body gives permission by asking the Can I? May I? and Should I? *questions.*

If permission is granted to all three questions, you have the energetic permission to impose. Set the antenna on the wavelength of the weak natural signal. Imposing brings the quality of the weak signal up to the quality of the signal emitted by the antenna by encouraging resonance.

The process of imposing to re-calibrate the energy body is identical to imposing to activate energy in an inanimate object. However, this time your intention is to open the flow of energy in either yourself or another person. The energy body of living beings manages itself by blocking acupoints, and when necessary closing an energy driver.

If you are particular with your questioning and, have the pure intention to only go where the energy can lead, at that point in time, and in that person's best interests, you cannot really go wrong. That said, I have come across people who assume that they have the right to interact and even intervene with someone else's energy for their own personal reasoning.

This is a gross misplacement of judgement. An example: '*my neighbour is a really difficult person, maybe I should just balance them*'.

It is unethical to interfere with the energetic
intelligence of the body without permission and
this is not associated in any way with
the ACMOS Method.

If someone does not approach you and explicitly give their permission, both verbally and intellectually, you have no right to influence their energy body. This consent is required over and above the energetic consent of Can I? May I? Should I?

Now that we have a clear understanding of the most ethical way to work, the energy will interact and inform your practise, to bring the best results possible in a given situation. The antenna is your tool to start opening up a whole new world of information. Use it well.

The energy can block for a variety of reasons and the protocol, appendix four of this book, will help direct to the most suitable and effective way to restore the flow.

This booklet covers basic energy balancing only.

Further study of the full ACMOS Method is recommended.

Energy may block due to:

- Incompatible objects on the body,

- An external threat, in which case the body temporarily disconnects a driver. It should re-open over time, but this process can often be shortened provided the threat signal has passed,

- A blocked area may be affecting the capacity of the whole to maintain its energetic connections e.g., after an injury when the thoughts may be dominated by pain, swelling,

- The cleaning capacity of the body may be overloaded. The lymphatic system may not be able to keep up with the speed of elimination. An example swollen and tender lymph nodes show the lymphatic system is working very hard processing when there is an infection in the body.

**CASE EXAMPLE:** If someone has a blocked cosmic driver 12, causing their 15.3 at the chest to block, and the 17.6 at the chest to block, what are the options after asking for permission to proceed to making a correction?

1. **Impose the blocked energy driver i.e., the 12.**

   Set your antenna on 12 and make the plus sign above their head whist targeting the top of the head. WAIT for the 12 of the cosmos to tune in with the person's 12. Although it is weak it is never totally absent. When resonance is established the cosmic 12 of the antenna 'turns up the volume' of the cosmic connection of the recipient. Their 12 comes back online and the antenna dips. If there is no response or the response is still weak, repeat this process until there is a strong dip when you test above their head.

   *Note:* When we are looking to create change, and we have obtained permission, both verbally and energetically, we CAN, in this situation, repeat the imposing process to strengthen the resonance. When testing we do not want to trigger a false positive with repeated testing, however when re-calibrating the energy we may need to repeat the process, to achieve a strong response.

   If the 12 unblocks slightly or does not unblock then the block is in place for a reason. We have some other options to enable the energy to re-establish flow.

2. **Check if the person is wearing an incompatible item which is blocking their energy.**

As beginners, it is a nice exercise to remove items and test them for 2.5. Metal items often lose their energetic quality over time, especially if worn continuously and may start to collect negative signals. Examples: rings, piercings, necklaces, glasses (metal hinges on glasses are worn near the brain).

Crystals, gemstones, and precious stones are widely used to promote health as they are thought to support and protect the energy in a variety of ways. Once these items reach their capacity or become 'full', they start to broadcast and influence your energy with the very energy you are using them to protect you from.

There is no need to become overly anxious about clearing metal items or crystals as you have an antenna.

With your antenna you can:

- Improve the energetic quality or clean the item or crystal

- Ask how long the re-charged state will last? Or alternatively when the item will need to be cleared again?

If the energy channel does not open after clearing check items which are removed daily, but which can be worn for long periods such as: buckles and shoes, followed by man-made items, especially if they circumnavigate the body – bras, belts, and bracelets. Once you become familiar with your antenna's response you can simply ask the question 'Is the person wearing a destabilising object?'. Then locate the object.

Not all metal items can be seen or even removed. Hidden sources of metal in the body can include plates and pins inserted to fix fractures, joint replacements, hidden piercings and hormonal or non-hormonal inserts such as intra-uterine devices.

If you cannot identify the object blocking the energy, subtly ask the person for more information. If the item cannot be seen you may still be able to clear it.

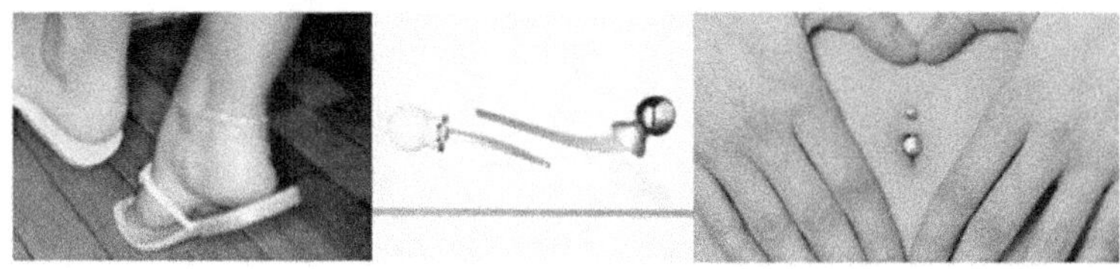

Although the actual item may be *inside* the person's body, their energy body can still guide you to a solution. Write the name of the hidden item in pencil on a white piece of paper and place it in their non-dominant hand — ask if you can correct the energy through this 'surrogate'.

Ask the person to hold the mass in their dominant hand whilst you ask if you can impose or clean an item on 2.5? Once you are more familiar with the process use appendix four, the antenna protocol to identify the *best* signal to strengthen *for that person* at *that point in time*.

# Chapter Fourteen:
## Analysis of Compatibility

THE MINIMUM RESONANCE COMPATIBLE WITH THE
HUMAN ENERGY SYSTEMS
IS **2.5** ACTU

Foods, supplements, items of jewellery and clothing can all affect a person's energy. We analyse the effect of these items by checking to see if they are compatible, and if they are not, we ask if we can change the energy of the item to make it more acceptable to the person's biofields.

### Analyse the Product First

If products do not resonate with 2.5 on the antenna they block the energy. Items which block our essential energy take more energy out of our working energy and our resources than they give us. They deplete us.

2.5 is the human cell harmony – Check the body for any articles which do not resonate at **2.5** as these are destabilising.

The energy body is very quick to respond when something destabilising is placed within the energy field. The **15.3** on the chest will 'cut' with the product in the non-dominant hand. If the person's **8** or the **12** is blocked, they will *not* resonate at **15.3** at the centre of the chest.

The personal environment of an individual, including objects such as: watches, jewellery, hidden items (e.g., piercings) within the energy field, can be blocking the energy.

Also, anything that is absorbed: foods, supplements, and externally applied products, must resonate at a minimum vibratory rate of **2.5**

ACTU to be energetically compatible with the human body. Anything which does not resonate at **2.5** may cause a block. We use this information to help make informed choices about foods, supplements, cosmetics etc.

2.5 is the human cell harmony – Check the body for any articles which do not resonate at **2.5** as these are destabilising.

We can impose the **2.5** with the antenna to energetically clean the product and make it acceptable to our body. Impose with the plus sign with the antenna set on 2.5

Recheck the persons energy readings – have they changed?

*Note:* Sometimes, things which are not compatible are also necessary, for example medications. Unless you are a medical qualified professional with appropriate training you cannot change a prescription medication.

If an item cannot hold the **2.5** after imposing — **ask** if this item is **17.6** *'negative'* with the antenna set on **17.6.**

17.6 negative is energetically destabilising. If a product resonates at negative 17.6, it is not compatible with humans, the product is polluted. It can be difficult or even impossible to clean. DISCARD the object or place it under running water then remeasure regularly. Check again later, as it is difficult for these products to hold their energetic quality.

*The exception to this rule is prescribed medicine*
***never interfere with a medical prescription.***

Measuring and imposing are done with the sliding cross- bridge set on the appropriate wavelength on the antenna scale however…

***All questioning*** *is done with the antenna set on* **17.6** ACTU (cord plugged into the right hole of the antenna).

Analyse the compatibility with the person second:

**First**: the vibratory quality of the product is tested on a neutral vibratory background e.g., a white sheet of paper. Once we know that the product has good energetic quality, we can assess the effect of that product on the energetics of the individual.

In order to make a comparison the Cosmo-Telluric (CT) channel must be open and resonant – when you measure 15.3 dips at the chest which means that the 8 and 12 are open or 'on' *and* that they are in balance with each other.

*One can only observe that the CT channel 'cuts' in the face*
*of a disturbing product if it was 'on' to start with.*

If the CT channel 'cuts' or blocks upon exposure to a product, it no longer resonates — the antenna no longer dips on **15.3** at the centre of the chest. There is an imbalance between the cosmic force and the earth force, influenced by the product held in the hand.

*Compatibility analysis* permits the selection of personal treatments or protocols:

1. Compatibility of supplements, with the person, can be determined by holding the product in the non-dominant hand, and checking the effect on the Cosmo-Telluric Channel, at the centre of the chest (**15.3**) Does the resonance remain open or 'cut' out?

2. With practise, multiple items can be held in the non- dominant hand to ensure compatibility between the combination of products and the individual. Check the Cosmo-Telluric channel at the centre of the chest (**15.3**)

   When checking multiple items, if the CT channel does not respond, it has cut. You should then check each product individually and in various combinations to find and check the best energetic solution for that person.

3.  Optimal compatibility and personalisation can be assessed, between *the individual* and *their products*. What is the optimum dosage, frequency, time of application and duration? How long they should take a supplement for maximum benefit? All of these can be determined by questioning with the antenna set on **17.6** whilst holding the product in the *non-dominant* hand.

    The energetic quality analysis chart, which is taught and supplied during the Lecher antenna training, refines the analysis process, and makes it simple to review change.

    *Be mindful of your level of training and do not recommend products or exceed the recommended daily dosage if you do not have a qualification to do so.*

*Tip*: in relation to people who take multiple supplements — Sometimes less is more. ☺

Looking deeper — The best products hold the 1.1 wavelength. This means the product is perfectly balanced and capable of opening the 1.1 gateway between:

- The surface energy (7.8 field)* where symptoms reside.

- And the deep energy (5.7 field)* where problems remain hidden, until such time as they impact the symptomatic surface field.

*These fields and their importance on global health and well- being are taught at the ACMOS Method international seminars or e-learning courses.

Although a product may hold the 1.1 'connecting' resonance, it may not be the ideal product, for that person, at that time.

Questioning becomes a true skill of the Lecher antenna user but like all new skills, questioning needs to be practiced. The most important thing is to practise regularly. If you use your antenna often, your accuracy and confidence will grow.

Specialised training gives the information required to ask highly informed questions – if you do not understand what you are asking, the energy will not give you the quality of response needed, for working at a deeper energetic level.

# Chapter Fifteen: Broadcasting

If you are in a space e.g. a hotel room or workspace where lots of people leave traces of their energy, the room may be unable to maintain its connection with the grand driving forces (8 & 12). Use the fifth column of the antenna protocol, appendix four, to assess which signal needs support.

To broadcast, sit the open antenna on top of the metal mass, with the slider set at the correct number and the arms locked in the open position. Ask where it is most efficient to place the antenna in the space. Set up the antenna, like a television aerial, with the slider set on **8, 12, 15.3 or 17.6** - ask the questions* Can I? May I? Should I?

The antenna will continuously broadcast the weak signal to the surrounding area and improve the quality of the space.

Another time it may be useful to broadcast is when you are unwell, for example if you have a viral infection. Supporting your energy channel as your immune system works hard to combat the infection may improve your recovery from the acute illness. Always ask which wavelength and how long!

## Important

Do not broadcast and balance at the same time as the broadcast may hide some deeper issues which could be resolved through the balancing process.

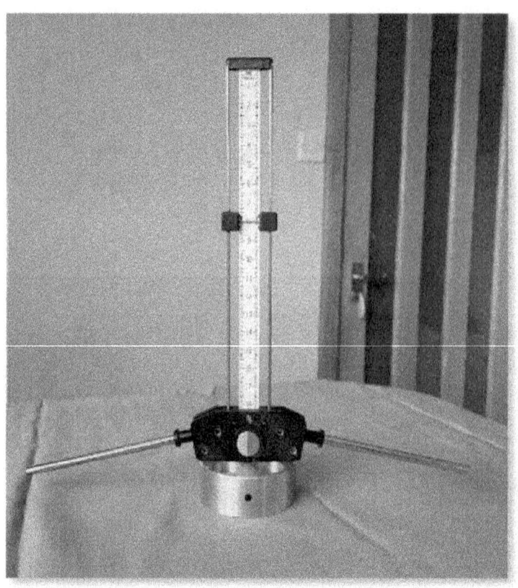

Always ask: When should I remove the broadcast?

Your body is always regulating itself and boosting a signal may not be required for long. It is not ideal to constantly expose yourself to a boosted signal.

When you consider the number of signals broadcasting in our environment today, you will understand that for most of the time the human body is capable of functioning well in the face of multiple signals.

It is important to understand this as it is possible to become afraid of signals, and as we cannot avoid them in this modern world, fear or anxiety does not benefit us. In fact these emotional responses deplete our energy significantly as we divert the resources of our bodies to being prepared for flight or fight.

I prefer to take a pragmatic approach and strongly believe in optimising the *natural connections* with the sun and the Earth, which have sustained life for billions of years.

By improving our own energetics we are better protected, in a position of more resilience, to adapt to environmental factors including signals with greater ease. Remember that the definition of true health is the ability to adapt to changing external and internal circumstances with ease.

# CHAPTER SIXTEEN:
# ANTENNA PROTOCOL FOR VIBRATORY BALANCE

Once confident you can use the following protocol.

1.  Check the channel of the *room* with the ACMOS Lecher Antenna at **17.6** ACTU.

    If there is no tension, it is possible to identify the fragile connection of the room by checking the **12** ACTU on the ceiling and the **8** ACTU on the floor.

    Restore the quality of the room by imposing the weak driver using the PLUS SIGN: use your antenna with intention and, state what you are trying to achieve.

    As an alternative you can open the space using a QuantAcmos light stimulator (see image) by making a plus sign using the pure white light.

    If the **15.3** ACTU is present but **not** the **17.6** ACTU, the room is not sufficiently ventilated. It is unable to clear stagnant energy or vibratory toxins due to lack of energetic flow. The room is likely to disconnect on either **8** ACTU or **12** ACTU, depending upon which one is weaker. Open a window or door.

2.  Check your *personal channel* on **15.3** ACTU on *chest* –short cut! Review Chapter nine.

    You should always make sure your own CT channel is *open* before working on anyone else. If your channel is not open, you will not be able to tune in with the problems of the person being tested. If there is no tension, reconnect your absent *driver* (**8** or **12**) or risk challenging the energetic connections of the individual that you are testing.

3. Assessing another person: Check the COSMIC CONNECTION above the person's head at **12** ACTU. If it is absent: **Ask** if it can be reconnected by imposing.

   Check the EARTH CONNECTION between the person's feet at **8** ACTU. If absent: **Ask** if it can be reconnected by imposing.

   Check the TENSION OF THE CT CHANNEL with the antenna set on **15.3** ACTU. Aim at the centre of the person's chest to confirm the balanced tension between the two grand drivers.

   If 15.3 is absent, either the 8 ACTU or the 12 ACTU is missing or weak. Feel the difference in tension (without repeatedly testing). Ask if the weaker driver can be reactivated by imposing. If not recheck the room and follow 4 below.

   *Note:* If the antenna does not respond, to either 8 or 12, the missing driver may need to be reset by carefully following a full ACMOS protocol which is beyond the scope of this book.

4. What can I do if the weak driver cannot be re-activated?

   If the driver has blocked as a protective reflex due to incompatibility with an object or item of clothing, ask whether something that the person is wearing is blocking their energy?

   Check for DESTABILISING ITEMS (p 31).

   Remove any metal objects and retest the **15.3** at the chest. If the 15.3 opens when an item is *removed* from the body that item was blocking the energy. Check the item at **2.5** — if there is no resonance, then impose the item with 2.5. Then give it back to the person and recheck their 15.3 – if it remains open then the item is now more compatible.

CHECK THE FIVE ENERGY CENTRES AT 2.5 ACTU — at the forehead, throat, chest, solar plexus, and sacral energy centres. The vibratory field shows the quality of the energetic management of each region and is measured at **2.5.**

Wherever the **2.5** ACTU is weak or absent, this indicates a block in the midline of the body at one of the main energy centres (chakras). If the weakness is in the upper, or in the lower part of the body, this indicates either a lack of cosmic or earth connection, respectively. Ask if you can impose the *weaker driver* which may open the blocked chakra – do not impose 2.5 directly at the energy centre.

The chakras are major control points. If opening a *driver* does not open the chakra an ACMOS protocol is needed to find and release the tension causing this block.

Check the **17.6** ACTU *at chest level* to confirm that the body is able to eliminate its vibratory toxins efficiently.

*Note:* This is the biological equivalent to the room blocking on **17.6** when the space becomes over-populated with old spent energy (vibratory toxins).

Check for ORGANIC ELIMINATION BLOCKS — (in the lymphatics) with **2.1** ACTU at three levels down each side of the body –underarm/axilla, waist, and groin (on both right and left sides). If any of the lymphatic areas respond slowly or do not respond then the lymph is becoming sluggish.

You can reactivate the lymphatic energy* by imposing 17.6 on the forehead whilst focussing your intention very clearly on the lymphatic system in your mind. *See column four on the antenna protocol – appendix four.

When the lymphatic system is optimised the body's system for cleaning debris, breaking down and recycling useful parts, and eliminating waste products is greatly enhanced.

Activating the lymphatics improves the overall efficiency of the working body to manage itself. It gives the person the best chance to improve the structure and function of their organs, tissues, and cells just as nature intended.

# Chapter Seventeen: Practical Measurements and Recording

## Putting Theory into Practise

### Measure the Quality of the Room

Is the **12** present?                    Where did you check?

What does the **12** mean?

Is the **8** present?                    Where did you check?

What does the **8** mean?

Is the **15.3** present?        Where?        Meaning?

Is the **17.6** present?        Where?        Meaning?

### Measure Yourself

**12, 8, 15.3, 2.5** x five places, **17.6** and **2.1**        Location on the body?
× six places What does the **12** mean?

Why do you measure 12 here?

What does the **8** mean?                    Location on the body?

Why do you measure 8 here?

What does the **15.3** mean?                Location on the body?

Why do you measure 15.3 here?

What does the **2.5** mean?                 Location on the body?

Why do you measure 2.5 here?

What does the **17.6** mean?                Location on the body?

Why do you measure 17.6 here?

What does the **2.1** mean?                 Location on the body?

Why do you measure 2.1 here?

Why do we use the non-dominant hand?

I suggest you write out your findings on a piece of paper. After a week or so of practise, repeat the exercise. Are you able to remember the answers to the above questions without looking at the booklet? Congratulations you are learning the language of your subtle energies.

## MEASURE OTHER PEOPLE - VIBRATIONAL MEASUREMENTS

Record measurements on the chart on the following page: tick or cross above the head for **12** ACTU, at the feet for **8** ACTU, five ticks or crosses down the midline for the five **2.5**s.

The boxes to the left of the figure are for the **15.3** (Cosmo- Telluric channel) and **17.6** (overall or 'global' vibrational balance). The 15.3 box is between the body and the 17.6

The circle at the centre of the chest is surrounded by oblique lines for the six lymphatic measurements. Cross the line if the area does not respond on **2.1**, put an O on the line for open if the antenna dips - lymphatic resonates at **2.1**.

17.6    15.3    8 12    2.5    2.1

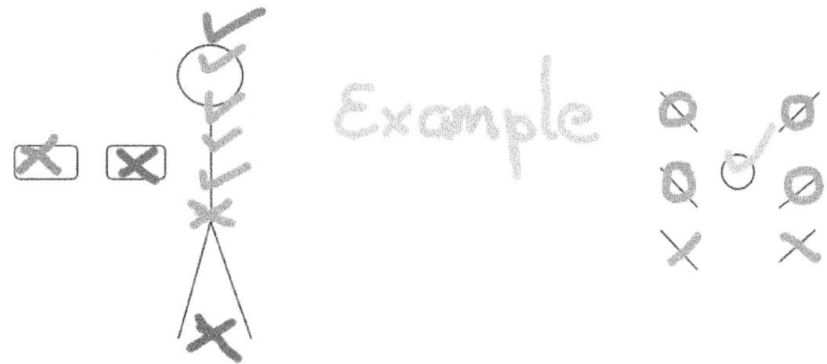

*Lymphatic quality in six places Axilla, waist, and groin on each side.*

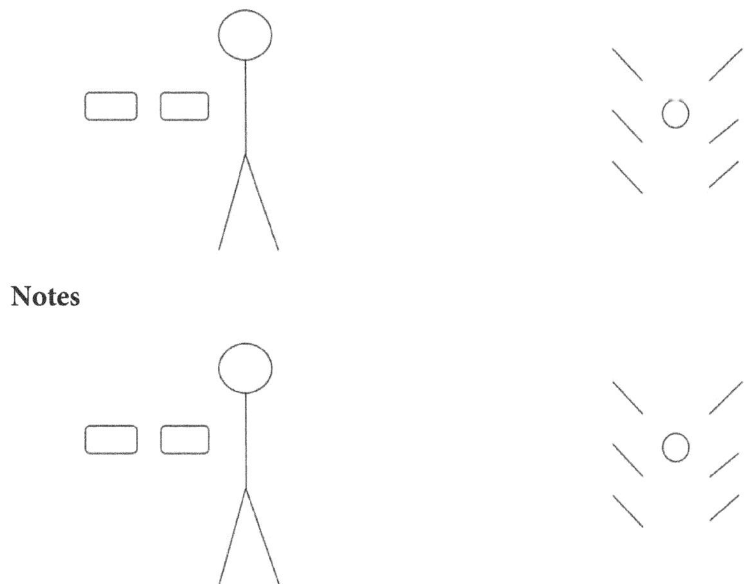

**Notes**

***Notes***: Remember that repeated testing can 'impose' the signal into the product so TRUST your initial answers.

MEASURING OBJECTS e.g., essential oils, rings, watches, fresh raspberries, bleach, artificially sweetened fizzy drinks, ... measure everything you can think of – PRACTISE.

## MEASURE THE QUALITY OF PRODUCTS

Repeat this process every day for a minimum of two weeks to gain confidence and accuracy). Write the name of the object in the top line. Cover your answers before you test each day. Think about what the numbers mean when testing then check chapter 7 the wavelengths.

| Name of object | | | | | | |
|---|---|---|---|---|---|---|
| **Test Date** | | | | | | |
| 2.5 | | | | | | |
| 8 | | | | | | |
| 12 | | | | | | |
| 15.3 | | | | | | |
| 17.6 | | | | | | |
| 1.1 | | | | | | |

Does the product have the minimum of **2.5**?

Why is this important?

What type of product is it? E.g., sedating?

Does holding the object in the non-dominant hand change the person's measurements?

Does it cut the channel – i.e., block the **15.3** at the chest?

If the **15.3** cuts at the chest the product is not compatible with that person – see the chapter on compatibility analysis.

## Find & Compare Several Plants in The Garden

Measure the plant energy on **3.8** Can you feel a difference in quality if you test a budding plant compared with a dying plant. Does the tension in the antenna feel different even if it moves for both plants?

Which plant has most vibrancy? More vitality or vital life force? Which has the least?

## Find Magnetic North

Stand facing a specific landmark. Put the slide of the antenna on 5.7 and slowly make a circle until the antenna moves. Mark an *x* on the compass below, at the point you find the antenna moves. Compare again on another day.

Most of all play with your antenna; explore the world around you, be inquisitive.

A word of warning though:

Do not become obsessed with measuring and do not measure the same thing too frequently, or you risk creating change without realising it.

Then your ability to discern, between a true reading and a reading you have inadvertently imposed, can cause you to lose confidence.

**PRACTISE EXPERIMENT ENJOY**

# A Note from the Author

Thank you for reading and especially for implementing the information in this very practical book. I give my heartfelt thanks to the Naccachian family and to my dear friend and colleague Widad Nash for their unwavering support. Also to Anny Luty and Tracy Hodge, my proofreaders and critiques par excellence.

And now to finish our journey I'd like to share a little of my story with you, and explain how I found a hidden pearl, this extraordinary niche.

I lived through eight years of absolute crippling fatigue – and came out the other side! In 1994, only 5 days before my wedding, I was diagnosed with a Hodgkin's Lymphoma. Staged at one, I was lucky, but the treatment proposed was radical in case the cancer had spread – the whole of my chest area and throat were irradiated over the course of 4 weeks, followed by 3 days intense targeted radiotherapy. The treatment saved my life, but… it also stole my health.

As a trained medical professional, it was difficult to be on the other side of the clinical fence. Throughout my journey I found the medical professionals to be both wonderful and humane, but also sometimes wanting. This lack was sometimes due to the shortage of time or funds, and nowadays is also affected by scarcity of services, or burnout in the staff.

But sometimes this is because the engrained thinking of the medical establishment holds back the boundaries to new paradigms. Whereas pharmaceutical companies and surgeons at hospitals, such as Papworth and Addenbrookes Cambridge, are allowed to push forwards the frontiers of 'pharmamedicine' and surgery – to save lives no matter the cost; the advent of 'evidence-based medicine' caused physiotherapists, and other health professionals in less clearly defined arenas, to turn on their peers.

'Where is your evidence?' became the banner to be upheld, and 'energy' was seen as a dirty word – a word unworthy of professionals - to be derided and sneered at. *Yet with no energy there is no life and with no life we are all out of a job!*

So, I have shared with you a little of my 'take' on energy in health, the vital force which illuminates our cells with life and gives us our inner compass, our purpose. The light which influences our experience of our lives and our health. True mind, body, and spiritual wholeness.

What are my credentials? I am a health professional with almost 40 years of experience in healthcare and well-being. When my health returned in 2002, I wanted to study whole of health and was particularly drawn to Chinese Medicine. In 2006 I came across ACMOS bioenergetics and learned at the foot of the master for 14 years. I continued to learn as part of the Association of Chartered Physiotherapists in Energy Medicine holding a variety of positions including chair.

I've been to many conferences, read lots of books, presented at international seminars, including the Quantum Energy Conclave II in Bangalore where I spoke as an innovator in the field of quantum medicine.

I have had many teachers over the past 40 years, none more so than my own journey… but my heart belongs to René Naccachian PhD, whose ACMOS Method lit a fire within me, transformed my life and the lives of my clients, and gave a framework to my understanding of energy as life. I taught alongside my mentor for 8 years and still grieve his loss today as I follow in the footsteps of a giant – this work is a tribute to my dear friend, Dr René.

*Carol Robertson, 2024.*

# Appendix One:
# Chart of Product Analysis

| PRODUCT ANALYSIS | Which wavelength does the Antenna respond to? |
| --- | --- |
| **Negative** product | **No response** to 2.5<br>Incompatible with humans |
| **Harmonic** product | **Response to 2.5**<br>Minimum quality for humans |
| **Sedative Yin** product | Response to 2.5<br>**Response to 8**<br>No response to 12, 15.3 |
| **Excitant Yang** product | Response to 2.5<br>**Response to 12**<br>No response to 8, 15.3, 17.6 |
| **Balancing** product | Response to 2.5<br>**Response to 8, 12**<br>No response to 15.3 |
| **Radiant** & harmonizing product | Response to 2.5<br>Response to 8, 12<br>**Response to 15.3**<br>No response to 17.6 |
| Radiant and **Regenerating** product | Response to 2.5<br>Response to 8, 12, 15.3<br>**Response to 17.6** |
| **Lemniscate** Perfectly balanced product | Response to 2.5, 8, 12, 15.3, 17.6<br>**Response to 1.1** |

Remember:

1.  Centre yourself through breathwork

2.  Check yourself with the drawer pulled out.

3.  Test items on a neutral surface such as a white piece of paper

4.  Connect the mass and place the mass on the paper.

5.  Place the item on the mass.

6.  Begin testing the energetic qualities of the item.

# Appendix Two:
# Lines of Defence

**FIRST LINE OF DEFENCE – level 1 energy imbalance**

Disorders begin at the vibrational level where the body defends itself by blocking either one of its global polarities (12 & 8)

As a disorder deepens, the body also blocks
the polarity of specific acu-points as it
attempts to manage the disorder*.

At this stage it may be possible to correct the energetic dysfunction with an antenna which will improve the energy flow to the area concerned.

The person may present imbalances which you have the capacity to 'reset' using your antenna by giving them the option to tune in with the natural driving forces of life. This may be sufficient to allow that person to restore their self-management capacities.

**Use the antenna:    set on 12 for cosmic
OR   set on 8 for earth**

*Therapists with appropriate knowledge can use their antenna to tune acupoints. Use 12 to stimulate and 8 to sedate the point.

---

**SECOND LINE OF DEFENCE – level 2 energy imbalance**

If an energetic disorder remains for a prolonged period of time or is particularly de-stabilising, then the body uses its second line of defence - it 'blows a fuse'. In this case, a full Acmos protocol is indicated and a practitioner needs the knowledge to access the Acmos range of harmonies, in order to: re-tune the signalling pathways which have been lost, remove negative signals which continue to destabilise the energy body, and restore optimum self-healing.

**This is the area of speciality of the Acmos Bioenergetics Practitioner.**

The ACMOS Method is a whole other level however good antenna skills underpin the application of the Method.

*ALWAYS REMEMBER:*

*Repeated testing can 'impose' the signal into the product so TRUST your initial answers.*

*New skills take time to learn and to embody.*

*There are a number of routes available if you would like to broaden your knowledge and feel more supported in your journey. We are here to help!*

# Appendix Three:
## Flowcharts for Measurements

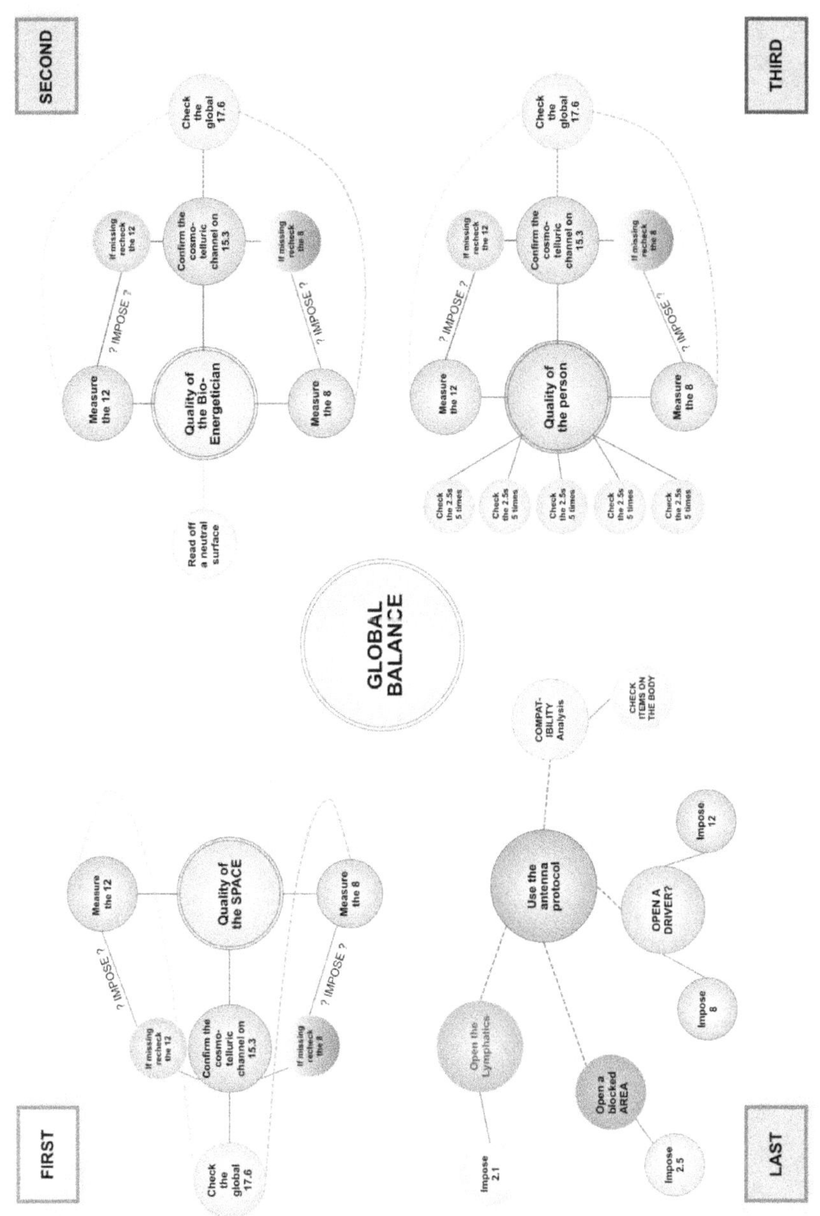

# Appendix Four:

## Antenna Protocol for Energy Balancing

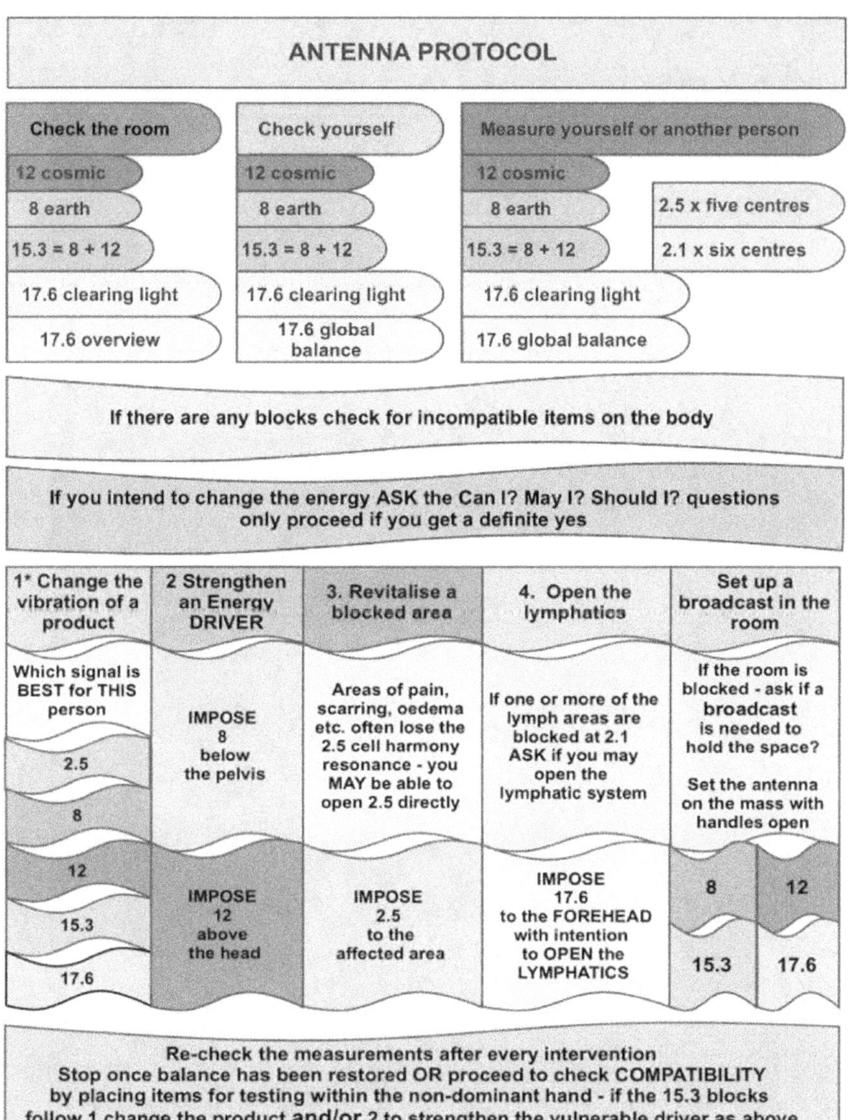


*Can I? May I? Should I? Respect the energy and the information it provides*

# Appendix Five: Next Steps

## Mastering the Lecher Antenna

Use our code **ROBE10** for a 10% discount.

https://me-qr.com/6aNVdPLk

## Buy your Lecher Antenna Here

Don't forget your discount code **ROB10INSTR** for a 10% discount at checkout.

https://me-qr.com/jepLy3k1

## Are You Interested in Learning More?

Visit: www.energymedicinetraining.com/courses/lecher-antenna-training-with-carol-robertson.